OUT OF EVIL

NEW INTERNATIONAL POLITICS AND OLD DOCTRINES OF WAR

Stephen Chan

I.B. TAURIS

LONDON · NEW YORK

Published in 2005 by I.B.Tauris & Co. Ltd
6 Salem Road, London W2 4BU
175 Fifth Avenue, New York, NY 10010
www.ibtauris.com

ISBN: 1 85043 420 4
EAN: 978 1 85043 420 7

A full CIP record for this book is available from the British Library
A full CIP record for this book is available from the Library of Congress

Library of Congress catalog card: available

Typeset in Goudy Old Style by A. & D. Worthington, Newmarket, Suffolk
Printed and bound in Great Britain by TJ International Ltd, Padstow, Cornwall

CONTENTS

PREFACE

On the Boulevard St Germain in Paris sits a café called *aux deux magots* and, seated in turn at an outside table at night, one can be entertained by fire-eaters and street theatre. Inside the café, presiding over a melange of tourists, wannabe philosophers and writers emulating Sartre and de Beauvoir who used to drink there, sit two carved statues of old Chinese gentlemen. These are the two *magots*. It takes a while to link the French words to the Biblical narrative. In John's book of Revelation, after the end of history and the advent of God's government on earth, the lieutenants of Satan - Gog and Magog - are released from imprisonment to test the faithful one last time. They launch a huge rebellion against God's throne, gathering many allies in their coalition, which, all the same, is doomed to failure. They are all thrown into the lake of ever burning fire - the Bible's first and only real description of the torments of hell. In the medieval manuscripts - everyone expecting the apocalyptic realization of these things early in their new millennium - Gog and Magog (the two Magogs, *les deux magots*) are shown as bestial devils, flying lizards, once-Godly creatures turned into the Godzillas of their day.

Hundreds of years later, the West having become more sophisticated, the two Magogs became Chinese - purveyors of an evil, corrupt and threatening civilization. Growing up Chinese, but outside China, I often used to wonder why so many people considered me somehow unclean.[1] And this seemed to assume a further dimension at the height of the rhetorical propaganda that was hurled in the 1950s and 1960s between Communist China and the West. I was very glad that Henry Kissinger went to Beijing in 1972 to begin the normalization of relations, although I later redeemed my brief admiration for him by a greater admiration for the opera *Nixon in China* by the great contemporary US composer John Adams, featuring a depiction of Nixon that was

vii

not altogether flattering. But, sitting outside at *aux deux magots* on a summer's night years ago, trying to avoid wine being spilt on me from the tight tables all around, dreaming as all young men do of being able to afford an apartment overlooking the Seine, I began to think that one day soon it would be the nations and people of the Middle East who would be demonized and seen as threats, flying destruction against the Western shores. Anyone or anything that rose up: lizards, Chinese, Arabs – it seemed a silly genealogy only at the time. And of course we and all our evil would be defeated and sent to the lake of fire burning with sulphur forever.

✠ ✠ ✠ ✠ ✠

The last 15 years of history have seen a tumultuous stream of questions. After the fall of the Berlin Wall in 1989 we all asked if there would now be peace in our time. Very shortly afterwards, with the first Gulf War and the first significant signs of contemporary Islamic discontents in the world, we asked if we were entering a new confrontation – not simply military and ideological, but military and theological. And, only a decade later, after 9/11, we asked what would happen next. Upon what quest did the US and the West so speedily embark? What is the Axis of Evil that the second George Bush described, in his State of the Union address of 1 September 2002, as a threat to the world? As the end of one presidential term overlaps with the beginning of another, the need for informed reconsideration of foreign policy has never been greater. The issues generated at the beginning of the twenty-first century cannot be solved by conquests, beleaguered occupations and expensive exits.

In this short book I begin not just with 9/11 and the War on Terror that was announced so shortly after. This was widened into a war against the Axis of Evil, so I have condensed the two terms into one, and called it a War on Evil. But, if war, and if evil, what sort of war and what sort of evil? How are these things defined and planned? It might seem that only 'evil' is the problematic term, but 'war' is in fact a highly problematic practice. So much of the last 50 years of Western history has been consumed by a drive to build scientific foundations for war: not just to develop nuclear weapons, but to develop a strategic doctrine in which they would be used - and this doctrine was proposed to be scientifically based, using games theory and probability theories. The mathematical chances of any scenario getting out of hand became something endlessly pored over and recalculated. Military thinking and political brinkmanship came to work together in a relationship that had not previously been possible.[2] It also made the calculation of losses possible: how many dead in a nuclear exchange before strategic control is lost? All this worked well, in theory, and in war-game simulations against Soviet armies and nuclear weapons, and as applied to conventional wars as well, but could it work against an unseen enemy? The problem since 9/11 is that, in fact, it *had* to work, since the US had no other military doctrine except that established on the scientific calculations of two highly technologized and rational antagonists. Rather than re-examine doctrine, the Bush administration thought that new technology would vindicate the old ideas. I begin my book with this history of strategic doctrine, for it has influenced greatly the War on Evil after 9/11.

As for evil, by its very nature it is intangible and thus needs to be given flesh and location. Seeking flesh and location, then applying science and military weight, might not be all that is required. And this 'evil': in what sense is there a clash between pure values, i.e. values that have decided not to live together, at least for a time, and which justify themselves in separate histories, philosophies and theologies? Are these values perhaps inadvertently Manichean - separating the universe into absolute good and absolute evil? If this is the case, then international understanding becomes a first casualty. What is called 'evil' is almost automatically beyond redemption, beyond discourse, beyond comprehension and understanding. I have tried in this book to reduce the absolute nature of what is proposed as evil. Understanding - and appreciation - need not be casualties.

And, finally, I have questioned what we call 'good'. Are we waging War on Evil for the moral cause of good? Or are we exercising power over 'evil'? Is power 'good', in the same way as 'evil' is assumed to be bad? This makes a short book a complex one. I have tried my best to write it simply. It is not an academic disquisition that the world now needs.

✠ ✠ ✠ ✠ ✠

The body of the text that follows was written in 2003. Much has hurtled forward since then. Vastly increased Iraqi resistance to foreign occupation has bogged the US and its UK allies in a cycle of bloodletting. After the Madrid train bombings a new Spanish government moved to withdraw its troops. But it was not only Madrid that signalled the internationalization of Iraq: foreign fighters have come to Iraq, determined to fight the US where they find it - now finding it conveniently nearer their countries of origin. No biometric passports are required to slip across the Iraqi border. But the bulk of the resistance seems to be Iraqi, and it has increased, not decreased, since the capture of Saddam. It is Iraqi prisoners who have been abused and humiliated by US warders in the jails that Saddam once used. If no other cultural research was undertaken for the US project in Iraq, those in charge of interrogation revealed an exact understanding of what most humiliates an Iraqi prisoner. For the most part US operations have been blunt. The resistance has grown almost as persistently as US tactics have remained heavy-handed. And the US has not been able to protect its own. The head of the provisional authority's governing council was killed by a suicide bomber in May 2004, and in that same month even the Pentagon favourite, the Iraqi politician Ahmad Chalabi, sought or was forced to reposition himself away from the US. This book enters production as the so-called transfer of sovereignty is about to take place in June, with a very difficult future in prospect.

Why then release a book whose prime case study is rapidly changing? The reason is precisely because the doctrine of war that was used in Iraq did not change, and the US has still not moved to develop an alternative. As Iraq festers and burns, Osama Bin Laden is still free and international terrorism is emboldened rather than defeated. It has in fact been given much room to grow as US resources have stretched themselves thin in Iraq. But the book seeks above all to illuminate the basic premise that good and evil are not easily distinguished, and they cannot be distinguished by making them separate - cleanly opposite. All the actors in the War on Evil are complex, certainly contradictory, and elude easy definition. And just as US strategic doctrine springs from an era of rationalized Cold War, so doctrines of resistance - even doctrines of terrorism - have origins of immense complexity. What I have tried to do in this book is to give a 'cook's tour' of some of this complexity, and have probably rushed through it all. It is not an academic book, and my academic colleagues may be horrified - both those who are specialists in the countries I have depicted, and those who are philosophers of good and evil.

But since I am indeed an academic by profession, if not always in skill, may I thank the School of Oriental and African Studies at the University of London, in which I work. The School's mission is to further our understanding of Africa and the Middle and Far East by teaching and researching their histories, cultures, languages, religions, laws and contemporary political and economic problems. Even the most ancient languages of Afghanistan and Iraq can be studied at the School. There is no other institution in the world with so much concentration, in literally one building, of expertise and commitment in these areas. I hope in my clumsy way I have been true to this mission. And I hope it is not too wretched a note to reveal that, both in the build-up to wars in Afghanistan and Iraq, and in the confused and terrible occupation of Iraq, the UK government made not a single approach to the School for advice or historical information.

PART I

WAR ON EVIL

1 FROM COLD WAR TOWARDS A NEW CLASH?

In the twentieth century the greatest wars were always between those who shared the same philosophical heritage. Germany and the Soviet Union were both, in different ways, European in thought, as was Britain. The legacy of European thought was highly visible in the United States. The great political, strategic and military contests came out of the same heritage, even if it was a broad heritage. During the Cold War, Karl Marx was read in the West as well as in the East. The Pacific War against Japan, however, was completed by technology to which Japanese military science had no answer. Wars in Korea and Vietnam were problematic - the opponents of the West thought in different ways to the West - but were still wars where the might of technology was brought to bear. The confrontation with China was difficult - Mao was inscrutable to understanding and prediction - but even China sought to answer the technological military might of the West with missiles and nuclear warheads of its own. No enemy of the West was declared a political enemy by virtue of being evil. They were sometimes, often consciously, *described* as evil, but it was not the notion of evil that dominated Western politicians and strategists. The arms race did. And no enemy of the United States ever actually attacked the mainland of the United States. If there was a description of evil it was evil at a distance, threatening to come closer certainly, seeking to sow seeds at home perhaps, but it had never actually landed on US soil with thunder and mayhem from the sky. In the years shortly before September 11 it was invaders from an alien universe that destroyed US cities from the air in films such as *Independence Day*, or a giant meteorite that was about to hurtle from heaven in a very bad film starring Bruce Willis.

So that on 9/11 - and in US folklore it will probably always be said like that, a pairing of numbers to make an infamous date

3

- the US, with its capacity to hurl missiles all over the world, had
two aeroplanes hurled against the Twin Towers of New York and
one against the Pentagon. In the shock and dismay that followed
- shock at the appalling casualties, dismay that the United States
had not been invulnerable - there was further wounded pride
over much of the international reaction. This seemed to say that
the United States had deserved the attack, or at least it now knew
how it felt to be on the receiving end, the direct implication
being that others had for too long been on the receiving end of
what the US had dealt out. In simple terms the reaction of the
US was to strike back where it could - to deal out once again its
own missiles of destruction - and the War on Terror found its
first target in Afghanistan. The succeeding war against the Axis
of Evil marched into Iraq, while gesturing pointedly also towards
Iran and North Korea.

There are two immediate questions raised by this short rendition. The first is: why was the US so surprised and shocked by
9/11, especially when so much of the rest of the world said that
it had it coming? The second is: why have the linked wars against
Terror and Evil been so little against transnational and secret
cells, not bound by borders, but against states with governments,
frontiers, armies and public life? This second question gives rise
to another: when a regime changes, something concrete has been
defeated and an audited victory can be declared. Are the new
wars of the twenty-first century, therefore, simply items in a
catalogue, or is a deeper understanding of the world being
avoided here? Is the United States, with its 'shock and awe'
technology of mass destruction, hoping for a technological
solution to the problem of what it calls evil?

I wish to address the second question, and those to which it
gives rise, later in this essay. A short note on the first question
might, however, be helpful at this point. It is not as if there had
been no warning signs. There were even what might be taken as
ever more ambitious rehearsals. There had been an earlier attack
on the World Trade Center itself in 1993, US barracks in Saudi
Arabia were bombed in 1996, US embassies in Nairobi and Dar
es Salaam were bombed (with greater loss of African than American life) in 1998, and the naval ship USS Cole was attacked in

2000. On 15 September 1999 the US Commission on National Security for the Twenty-First Century - a bipartisan group - released a report entitled *New World Coming*. It had a prophetic first conclusion: 'The United States will be attacked by terrorists using weapons of mass destruction, and Americans will lose their lives on American soil, possibly in large numbers.'[1] On 31 January 2001 the Commission warned the new president, George W. Bush, to initiate preparations to deal with such attacks. Little was done, and the Twin Towers fell on 11 September that year.

Members of the Commission based their reasoning on what were becoming widely held strands of thought in the academic and think-tank worlds of international relations, outside the confines of the Pentagon and the closed ranks and ever tighter circles surrounding the White House. There were four main interlinked strands of thought. One: globalization has meant an internationalization of markets and finance. Two: it has also meant a transnational explosion of information and information networks. Three: there has been a concurrent weakening of already weak nation-states, particularly those artificially created by the era of colonialism. Four: the weaker such states, the greater the seedbeds they provide for terror cells to wreak a new form of war. The implication here is that the new form of war - war by terror - would be wreaked against the masters of global markets and finance. In this sense of course the attack against the World Trade Center was both symbol and proof of this last strand of thought. There are, however, certain difficulties with all four strands.

Firstly, the globalization of finance provides a complex web for all manner of transactions. Added to this there has developed a parallel informal web of global movement of currencies, and the two webs intersect in complex launderings and hidden accounts. What is called terror depends on the existence of globalized financial systems as much as the formal institutions of the United States and the West. Secondly, global communication and information systems provide for terror exactly the sort of organizational resources that are required by formal Western institutions. If terror now uses aeroplanes, explosives that can demolish city blocks and punch holes in warships, and is suspected of wishing to use biological and chemical weapons, terror is now scientific and technologized, accesses information and plays an electronic game of cat and mouse with Western surveillance. Thirdly, not all 'artificial' nation-states are weak: 'regime change' in Iraq was deemed necessary by US planners precisely because the regime was so strong. The same might be said of North Korea in the future (and North Korea is an artificial creation at least to the extent that it is one-half of what was a larger state). States may have been artificially created as a result of colonial borders, but many have established strong projects of nationalism that draw on centuries, if not millennia, of at least tangentially connected history. All of Saddam Hussein's rebuilding of Babylon was not entirely to do with his personal vanity and evil. As for the weak state of Afghanistan, the Taliban probably imposed a stronger government than its modern predecessors, and Osama Bin Laden did not come to Afghanistan because its government was too weak to prevent him from doing so, but because its government was strong enough to welcome him to stay. There was a deliberate policy-oriented invitation to Osama. So that, fourthly, the war of terror against the United States is not reducible to the weak warring against the strong, the fragmented warring against the global. It may be that there are, in a truer equation, competing visions of what should be global. But the secular strands of thought enumerated by members of the Commission on National Security for the Twenty-First Century echo the technological vision of how to answer the world's challenges that has always been part of the core of US foreign and defence policies. And perhaps the Commission wished to avoid repeating the more banal reductionisms of Samuel Huntington's *Clash of Civilizations*.[2]

This book of 1996, and its short predecessor article of 1993 – particularly the 1993 article – created a huge wave of largely uninformed and speculative thinking: that the West and its values were under challenge, that Western values had to be cherished and defended, that 'other' values, those doing the challenging, were alien and somehow improper, that the West should draw a line in the global sand across which these improper values should not cross, and that the world would become, in this sense, bipolar once again, with values and their host countries firmly marked (and separated) on an immediately discernible geopolitical map of the world. The challenging values were taken to be largely Islamic.

The upshot, at least in the minds of crude strategists, was that a geopolitical identity could be given to an oppositional value. Changing the regime of a country was somehow tantamount to changing, at least ameliorating, the values that were contained in that country. The questions of the content of those values, what they meant, why they were held, how they spread beyond boundaries, how they influenced governments as much as they were used by governments, how they anchored nationalisms and had a view of internationalism, were not deeply asked. But this does help, at least, the beginning of an explanation as to why, after 9/11, a popular view developed that a War on Terror or a War on Evil somehow was also a stand against the encroachment of Islam. And this was Islam in caricature, at best in huge generalization, without nuance and without inquiry. And it was an Islam that, within its host geopolitical states, could be bombed into submission with the weapons of a very great technology.

I said that it was the beginning of an explanation, but it is only a beginning. This essay is itself merely a nod in the direction of complex understanding, but what it will seek to do in the pages that follow is to:

- make a brief statement about the nature of evil in the history of Western thought;
- discuss the Cold War in Western terms to do with the predominance of strategic doctrine rather than ideological images;
- note the intrusion of the question of Iran into the second part of the Cold War;
- comment upon the brief rise of an 'end to history' with the apparent victory of Western liberalism and its values;
- comment on the 'dogs in the manger', with Islam involved in the seemingly intractable wars of Israel and Palestine, and in the Balkans, and the rise of the thesis that a 'clash of civilizations' loomed;

- note the lack of political preparedness and military planning for the onslaught of 9/11;
- comment on the expedition into Afghanistan, against the backdrop of that country's modern history, and the origins of international fighters such as Osama Bin Laden;
- comment on the invasion of Iraq, against the backdrop of that country's post-colonial history and the nature of government under Saddam Hussein;
- postulate the difficulties of any future war against Syria or Iran;
- warn against the terrible costs of any future war against North Korea;
- warn against a theology that has entered Western foreign policy, in which the struggle against evil has replaced the struggle for political objectives, in which evil is thought able to be overcome by technological and military might, and in which a monoculture finally bestrides the world in what can only prove to be a Pyrrhic Pax Americana.

Monotheism

The problem with a doctrine of one God is that He (or She) becomes responsible for all things, both good and evil. The authors of the book of Genesis sought to circumvent this problem by making the Serpent, the woman, then the man admit evil into conscious life. This was done by eating the fruit of the tree of knowledge of good and evil. Humanity thus chose its own corruption and, if a spiritual agency was involved in the choice, it was not God's. This was neat, but it was still God who created the tree of knowledge of good and evil, who proposed the test of temptation, who created the Serpent and who created the capacity first for temptation and second for recognizing evil when finally it could be seen. It was God who was responsible for a dualism implicit in creation, which was merely made explicit by the Serpent and wayward humanity. This dualism has sat at the heart of the Judaeo-Christian tradition since its inception.

By this I mean chiefly since the Gospel attributed to John. The Jesus of that Gospel has a very different provenance to his counterpart in Matthew, Luke and particularly Mark. Mark's is a curiously human Jesus, but all three portray a birth and death that is merely miraculous. The beginning of John is truly cosmic in its scope. It did not make a statement about creation, but proposed its methodology. Existence appeared not just because God created it but because Jesus, as the *Logos*, the Word, articulated it. That this same Articulator of the entire universe should become flesh simply did not chime easily with what all humanity knew about the limits of flesh. The difficulty of the divine amidst what was human was a backdrop writ large in John. Moreover, the Revelation, also attributed to John, has Jesus restored after death to cosmic splendour and, if ever there was sustained and dramatic metaphor of what cosmic power meant, then it was in the Revelation. The first Christian dualism, therefore, was not simply between good and evil – as it was in the Judaic canon – but between what was human and what was divine. Augustine, writing much later, constructed what remains an essential theology in which the City of God is counterpoised to the city of men.

Augustine, however, had emerged from Gnostic and Manichean influences. At his point in time his writings became decisive. Mark's had been the earliest Gospel (about AD70) and portrayed the most fleshly Jesus. Matthew's and Luke's were probably written ten years later, but John's appeared as late as AD100, and his highly charged sense of cosmic creation and struggle prefigured – if it was not actually an early part of – the Gnosticism that flourished from 100 to 200, and which was still highly influential by the time of Augustine (354–430). Without the intervention of Augustine, Christianity would have had a very different sort of dualism at its heart, but even now the Gnostic and Manichean 'heresies' (as they came to be called by the established church) retain a subcultural influence on Christian discourse.

From 100 onwards, many other gospels were written, but none was added to the canon of Matthew, Mark, Luke and John. In fact, the 'truth' of the gospels – which were truthful and which were not – was part of an immense power struggle within the early church.[3] At stake was an orthodox and Judaic view of monotheism (and, by extension, a single, undisputed church leadership). However, the Roman Empire bestrode a much wider world than Israel ever had, and all manner of mystical influences bore down upon it, including those of Persia and India. From within, the influence of neo-Platonism, developed from Plato's views of the spiritual and the ideal, was also strong. The victory of the orthodox allows us to call today's heritage Judaeo-Christian whereas, if Christianity had been allowed to develop in a cosmopolitan manner, it would have contained both greater pluralisms and different dualisms. Different Gnostic writings, some claiming to have also been written by John, talked of God as both male and female; of the God of the Garden of Eden as a local provincial God, anxious not to be challenged by creation if it came to knowledge; of a path to God that consisted in personal mystical union, not via the sacrifice of only one being, divine or not; and some came to talk about the dualism of good and evil – responding to the view that a good God could not create evil – and spoke of twin Gods, or at least of twin spiritual principles within the universe. This is what came to be called Manichean-ism.

It was Manicheanism that survived the various purges of the church, so that it continued periodically to raise its head. In the Middle Ages this was particularly the case. The Paulicians of seventh-century Armenia, the Bogomils in the Balkans of the tenth century, the Albigensians (or Cathars) of twelfth- and thirteenth-century France and Italy all had implicitly or explicitly within their teachings the idea that there were two Creators, one of good and one of evil. What the orthodox church has done, over the many years of such challenge, has been to develop and refine early Judaic images of the devil, or Satan.[4] If there are two spiritual principles within the universe, one of them is not a God equal to the other, but fallen (though he had indeed sought to depose God by waging war against Him) and, as a result, damned. Heretics burned at the stake were accused of being followers of Satan. The universe was not dualistic, in the sense that God and Satan were not equal. It was dichotomist, in that Satan's struggle against God continued to be fought on earth – having been lost in heaven – so that the world at least contained good and evil (but good was destined to win). This became a mainstream view within orthodox Christianity, and accommodated (unsatisfactorily) within it the various earlier senses of dualism. However, ideas of personal union with God remain, and even the idea of Satan as somehow noble – an epitome of the doomed human struggle against omnipotence – has remained. Milton's Lucifer, Blake's depiction of Lucifer rousing the fallen angels, Burne-Jones's painting of a defeated Satan rather calmly leaving heaven (and modelled on his earlier painting of St George), all these have the resonance of a time when good and evil were, or aspired to be, co-existent and equal. The orthodox discourse of today, however, is still swift to make use of a dualism in which good and evil exist, but good is heavenly and evil is ignoble and bad, treacherous like the Serpent in Eden, rebellious like Satan in heaven, fallen and doomed to fall further as in the most literal readings of John's Revelation.

Cold War

All of this can be directly, but crudely, applied to diagnoses of recent history and the various discourses – or at least vocabulary – used to demarcate historical epochs. Thus, if now we have a War on Evil, we had an Evil Empire during part of the Cold War – as the Soviet Union was stigmatized in the soundbite politics of the United States. That, however, is precisely the point: at some stage it became soundbites and, even in early full-blown ideological mode diabolical images of the Soviet Union never eclipsed efforts at rational planning and armament. Thirty-five years ago the analyst Ralph K. White wrote that misperceptions as well as perceptions of an enemy were always possible in strategic planning, but very few of these misperceptions were to do with a view merely of the enemy being diabolical. He gave six forms of misperception:

- a diabolical enemy image
- a virile self-image
- a moral self-image
- selective inattention
- absence of empathy
- military over-confidence.[5]

Of course, today's social theorists would say that the first
three in White's list are interdependent. One must have a view
of an 'other' if one is to have a view of self, and usually the
'other' is seen in a lesser and contrary light to oneself. Even so,
construction of an 'otherness' sits alongside the more purely
political, moral, and military considerations in the second part of
White's list. It was not enough simply to say the enemy is a devil,
the enemy is evil. Indeed, as the years of the Cold War wore on,
the construction of discourse to justify confrontation, to justify
constant armament and latest-generation armament, became
more and more sophisticated, less and less to do with diabolical
images of the enemy, and more to do with strategic calculations
and how to stay ahead of an enemy also racing to become more
sophisticated and more highly technologized than the United
States military.[6]

All the same, it would be ahistorical to say that in the 1950s
there was not a mood of anti-Communism in much of the
United States. The McCarthy witch-hunt for those suspected of
having Soviet sympathies – even though it got so overblown that
the White House could not wait for the fall of McCarthy – and
much popular entertainment painted an image of the US under
siege, not only from without, but from Communist sympathizers
within. The now deceased comic hero Captain America, dressed
in clingfilm stars and stripes, performed his gymnastic contor-
tions against slimy, fat and 'Russian'-looking villains with names
like Rhode Island Red, rather precisely identifying where the
McCarthy right suspected the epicentres of Communist conta-
gion to be. If there was an induced psychology of
misapprehension in much of the public mind, abetted by real
fears of nuclear destruction – as the reality and power of the new
weapons began to sink in, as well as the fact that the Soviets had
acquired them too – this was, again, insufficient to support a
strategic doctrine or to justify a rush to war. Indeed there was no
rush to war. There were rumours of possibly imminent war but,
once again, not to allay any psychological disquiet about the
diabolical nature of the Soviets. The pioneering strategic analyst
Bernard Brodie wrote that there were six contemporary theories
of war causation – only one of them psychological. These were:

- economic theories
- scandal school (what he termed Marxist) theories
- military–industrial complex theories
- special case of oil theories (this was 30 years ago)
- psychological theories
- political theories.[7]

To these should be added (as Brodie did in his wider writings) the idea of strategic doctrine being a possible cause of war. The first coherent US nuclear strategic doctrine was announced on 12 January 1954 by the Secretary of State, John Foster Dulles. He spoke of 'massive retaliatory power', on which the US would 'depend primarily', putting faith in 'a great capacity to retaliate instantly by means and at places of our own choosing'.[8] Dulles was speaking of a primary reliance on nuclear weapons, and the broad rationale could be described as follows:

1. There was a need for economy in US defence. In Dulles's words the US did not wish 'to fight in the Arctic and in the tropics, in Asia, in the Near East and in Europe; by sea, by land and by air; by old weapons and new weapons', attempting to match the enemy 'man for man, gun for gun and tank for tank'. There was thus to be a concentration on the most effective and efficient weapons.
2. There was a need to deliver a warning to the Communist world in the aftermath of Korea that US interests should not be challenged again, since overwhelming technological (nuclear) responses would be available.
3. There was a desirability in putting forward a threat that could not be matched by the Soviets (who had not then developed nuclear weapons), thus giving the US not only a sense of security, but a massive leverage in the conduct of international relations. The Soviets would be placed on a constant defensive.

There was great logic and rationality in all this. The weakness, however, lay in its application. It was a question of credibility. Would the Communist world believe it – believe that the US would use a sledgehammer to stop perhaps the bite of a flea? Would it use nuclear weapons to fight guerrillas? And if it refrained from using nuclear weapons against one 'flea', how emboldened would many 'fleas' then feel in many parts of the world – in all those parts Dulles sought to avoid? With many fleas biting and no nuclear response deemed appropriate, who would be on the defensive then?

The Dulles doctrine was further weakened when the Soviets did finally develop their own nuclear capability. Once the Soviets had enough nuclear weapons of their own, they too could unleash massive retaliation at times and places of their own choosing and exercise leverage in international relations. The US recognized this was happening, and the idea of an arms race became embedded in defence planning. However, it was not simply an arms race at nuclear level. Very many policy makers and strategists began urging the abandonment of an economic and efficient defence policy (i.e. a prioritized nuclear one) in favour of defence capacity across the board, from conventional to nuclear, not quite man-for-man and tank-for-tank, but sufficient to meet a Soviet threat at any level. These across-the-board strategists may have seemed hawkish in their day, advocating massive increases in defence spending, but they were also dovish in the sense that they were hoping to turn the US from a primary reliance on nuclear war.

The critics of Dulles also pointed out the difficulty of locating what was meant to be a doctrine of deterrence in only one sort of weaponry. One sort of weaponry could not meet all possibilities and all contingencies. More than that, however, what began to emerge was a new sense of strategic possibility. It was considerably more nuanced and claimed to be more realistic than previous thought. The new strategic thought abandoned the idea of victory; it even abandoned the idea of shrinking what was controlled by the enemy – of 'rolling him back'. The idea was that multi-level weaponry capacity and strategy would *contain* the enemy. If deterrence was involved, the enemy would be deterred from expanding beyond set frontiers and limits. The enemy was not to be deterred from taking no action at all; it was recognized that he too had interests and sought to guard them; he could not be made to feel on a constant defensive about them.

> We give up the concept of victory in its traditional meaning. We discard the idea of punishing aggression. We accept limits on our military and general policy objectives, and, in effect, we accept existing political and territorial arrangements.[9]

To a remarkable extent when, at the end of the twentieth century, we look at Samuel Huntington's 'clash of civilizations' thesis and the idea that it spawned that there should be a line in the global sand, separating the West from the world of Islam and, on either side of this line, both sides could just get on with their values and their modes of society, neither interfering with the other, we can see its ancestor in the liberal strategic thought of the late 1950s and early 1960s. When, at the beginning of the twenty-first century, political figures like US Secretary of Defense Donald Rumsfeld are taken to speak of a huge US hegemony over all of international relations, we are perhaps looking at a more complex reincarnation (for more complex times) of John Foster Dulles. We shall return to this theme later in the essay.

For now, returning to the Cold War and what was to become its next stage of development, the departure of Eisenhower from the US presidency and the eclipse of the Republicans and Dulles brought a new generation of Democrat 'whizz kids' to Kennedy's Washington. The liberal strategists never became the first tier of administration in the *faux* Camelot of that era, but they did occupy a great deal of Defense Secretary Robert MacNamara's second tier. More than that, on the other side of the Atlantic bright young politicians such as Denis Healey in the UK and Helmut Schmidt in Germany were writing books on the need for 'graduated deterrence' – what the US would soon call 'flexible response'. After all, if war with the Soviets came, Europe would likely become a major battlefield. The new political generation wanted to envisage their world as one in which city after city was not predestined to become Hiroshimas and Nagasakis.[10] On the US coast of the Atlantic, however, such search for graduated levels of deterrence – and, if need be, escalation – and for a flexible range of response gave birth to an illiberal monster. The monster was sired, however, for the best of liberal reasons: to avoid nuclear war as a first and only resort.

Flexible response seemed a rational alternative to massive retaliation: a response would be made available for each and any level of provocation; as provocation built, there would be a corresponding build-up of response; response would thus proceed through graduated phases of conventional war to nuclear war; even at the level of nuclear war, there would not be massive retaliation, but nuclear war could itself be flexibly graduated according to the provocation – damage inflicted would be proportionate to the size of the offence and thus be 'acceptable damage'. This would somehow be less dangerous and somehow more moral – so it was not a life for an eye, but an eye for an eye. In the corridors and think-tanks of Camelot there was a curious Old Testament echo in the new strategy. Nothing to do with evil, everything to do with precise requital. In summary, the new strategy looked for:

1. a punishment at the same level as the offence
2. a warning against repeating or escalating the offence
3. a signal that there was room to disengage and negotiate before a further escalation, both of offence and response.

It was this last point that contained a huge assumption. It said that there were separate steps on the way to full-scale nuclear war. There were therefore as many opportunities to disengage as there were to escalate. Thus if you bomb Aberystwyth in Wales, I do not bomb Moscow but look for the Soviet equivalent of a Welsh coastal town with a good university department of international relations. When I find it and bomb it, you can either say, 'Right, we'll raise the stakes and take out Wolverhampton', or you can say that enough damage has already been done and ask to talk. The opportunity to talk continues to reappear at each stage until you have bombed London, and what is left of me seeks at last to take out Moscow.

The assumption was that the enemy would be as rational as the responding side. This also throws an onus on the responding side to declare itself, to ensure that the enemy does not misunderstand its intentions and signals. The extent of one's retaliatory capacity has to be revealed. It cannot be kept secret. It has to say, 'Look, we really can respond and escalate our response all the way from Odessa to Moscow.' Not only was military might no longer aiming for traditional victory, but it revealed its plans. The belief in rationality – under nuclear fire – and the sense that naked diplomacy would be possible under this sort of fire was staggering. The advent of theatre or tactical nuclear weapons, smaller and mobile weapons that could be used on battlefields to take out a massed army or even a tank squadron rather than a big city, lent encouragement to this sort of thinking, except that it soon became not just an eye for an eye, but a pawn for a pawn.

The most famous or infamous rendition of such strategic scenario-building was given by Herman Kahn. A think-tank academic, his work was either tremendously influential in defence circles, or very reflective of thought in those circles. In his 'ladder of escalation', he proposed 44 steps of escalation, each step (until the last) being also a step in which reflection, pause and negotiation were possible. The 44 steps were divided into seven groupings, beginning with 'Subcrisis Maneuvering' and ending (literally) with 'Civilian Central Wars', in which the last step was named 'Spasm or Insensate War'.[11] At the time, even Helmut Schmidt approved of Kahn's work. The various steps all assume (a) a set of controllers on both sides who are immune to the actual warfare, and who (b) remain perfectly rational and cold-blooded in the face of escalating excesses, (c) that steps are not opportunistically jumped, and that (d) the public is insensate from the beginning, a lump of citizenry to be traded in, without clamour, at each responsive, flexible and appropriate rung of the long ladder, which, all the same, might seem a horrifically short ladder in the actual heat of escalation, destruction and wantonness.

Although today Kahn's ladder seems both optimistic and horrendous – the two forming a certain naivety – what it represented was the beginning of an approach to strategy and war based on calculation. In the late 1960s Anatol Rapoport introduced an edition of Clausewitz's classic on Napoleon's campaigns with an essay on games theory. It had almost nothing to do with Clausewitz's concerns, but everything to do with the new vogue in strategy.[12] In short, with the technology of destruction had come the technology of thought.

This was not something confined to foreign and defence policy. The idea of social engineering, the interest in sociological measurements, the enthusiasm for what the new British prime minister of the 1960s, Harold Wilson, called 'the white heat of a technological revolution', the new functional and linear architecture, all articulated an almost Victorian self-belief – substantiated by science, the applications of science and scientific thinking. In the emerging academic discipline of international relations a fierce debate arose as to whether its inquiries could be best conducted by historically based but somewhat intuitive scholarship, or by the new social scientific methodologies and the new tools of prediction.[13] What was meant by a 'tool of prediction' was, most basically, games theory – that, as in any game with gains or losses, even the losing player would seek to reduce how much he or she lost; that the most pleasant game was where both players could somehow win; and the most stable game was where neither lost. Each player at any stage of a game had options from which to choose – each option taking into account the likely response from the opposing player. It was a little like chess, and, like chess, various options, like various pieces on the board, could be assigned values (a rook was more valuable than a pawn). The trick was to command the board, but not deny the opponent some values. Neither side wanted the game to end, since a new game – if one were possible – would have to start with equal values on both sides. If this were not so, and a crushing victory was won, the entire defence-strategy industry and culture would have to change. Instead the idea was to be always one step ahead of the opponent in an ongoing game, to predict the opponent's moves based on the pieces left on the board and the values they represented. The game could not be allowed to end, i.e. the king could not be checkmated, but seizure of a queen and rooks would seriously weaken the opponent's ability to attack. Thus, although neither player was made to lose, the trick was to ensure that the other side could never win, and that you commanded the greater number of values.

There are two assumptions here. The first is that both players not only play by the rules but play rationally – the more a player can plot the game, as if by computer, the better. The second is that both players have something like equal skills. To this might be added a third assumption: that both players have equal temperaments. No one was going to storm out of a match or, worse, take a swing and deal out a black eye before storming out. Like chess, it was a game suited for two players. In international politics, the world had to be bipolar. One of the reasons why Henry Kissinger visited China in 1971 and brought Nixon with him in 1972 was to arrive at a rapprochement with China that allied China more with the US than the Soviet Union, and certainly to reduce China's role as a maverick third player in the finely balanced bipolar world that Kissinger sought.[14] For, although side games could be played with other actors, the main game – with its gambits, reciprocities and constant weighting of values – could best be played by two. It should be said, however, that both Kissinger and the Chinese premier, Zhou Enlai, discerned pretty accurately – even down to the nuances – exactly what values were held dear and which could be traded by the other. Kissinger enjoyed his negotiations with Zhou so much that he might have wished that China, not the Soviet Union, was the main player opposite.

It is, however, the fine appreciation of opposing values that makes a good game work. In the assignment of mathematical value to each step possible in the other side's deployment, the mathematics often cannot reflect values that may be extra-rational, i.e. outside received rationality but perhaps within a different rational system, or simply irrational. The leading British scholar on games theory and other forms of rational decision-making processes in international affairs, Michael Nicholson, developed a sensitive approach to how these techniques of analysis might be deployed, taking into account paradoxes, emotions and the warping of rationality.[15] However, many if not most users of games theory have no such sensitivities. And they certainly do not, as Nicholson did not, take into account the fact that different cultural backgrounds could introduce variabilities in the construction of rationality and the ascription of value.[16]

Martin Hollis and Steve Smith published a balanced and polished account of 'the games nations play', and theirs is a view of games theory consonant with Nicholson's. However, they do give a brief but very insightful account of the 1986 US bombing raid on Libya.[17] I said earlier that side games can be played, but they should not interfere with the main game. The US bombing had nothing to do with a bipolar world, and Libya was regarded sufficiently as a maverick to be well off the Soviet and any other view of the chessboard. More than that, however, the US raid seemed to have no true strategic rationale. Why start a side game for no good reason? In the UK prominent authors saw the raid as the act of 'mad dogs'.[18] The US justified the raid as a retribution against acts of terror which it said had been committed or sponsored by Libya (it since turns out that most were probably sponsored by Syria). Even if Libya had been a patron of terror, as Hollis and Smith point out, the raid would still have been outside the provisions of international law. Moreover, although the US action was 'rational' in terms of a domestic ploy to placate domestic opinion, Hollis and Smith advance a number of carefully modulated but still powerful reasons as to why it was peppered with irrationalities when its official account was laid alongside European and Arab views and sensitivities on the matter. Here Hollis and Smith's account and analysis stops. What might be said, however, is that the US sought to present their actions as rational, against the backdrop of the assumption that President Qaddafi's rule was persistently irrational. He did not play by the rules of the game and, if he had other rules which he valued, these were of no account to the US. Indeed few even in the Arab world were disposed to engage in lengthy defences of the rationality of Libyan policies.

John Davis, however, wrote a widely ignored but nonetheless superb study of the cultural and historical roots of Qaddafi's Libyan revolution.[19] This was published a year too late (in 1987), but it illustrated the complexities that form what others see as an irrationality. Today Qaddafi merely seems eccentric, but he was more, if differently, rational in 1986 than the US gave him credit for. This is neither the time nor place to launch an exposition of Libya and Qaddafi. However, there is a warning note that can be redirected to the later core of this essay, and that is to do with the *assumption* on the part of the US that *its* actions are necessarily rational, even if only because they seem so domestically, because the technology that implements its policy must be operationalized in a scientific and rational manner.

The side show with Libya, with the poor critical ratings it received from Europe and the Arab world, also suggests why what has been called the Second Cold War treated Third World countries not as independent actors with their own values but as proxies or pawns of the Soviet Union,[20] so that, although the US was engaged in foreign policy actions in many places, its international doctrine remained bipolar. It was still the US vs the Soviet Union in the Reagan years of the 1980s that spawned this second phase of the Cold War.[21] The Second Cold War followed upon the ending of the First - when Europe and its confrontation with the Soviet Union had stabilized in a series of understandings and commitments. After Europe there was the wider world - without the huge complication of China and Vietnam - and that wider world was a place where lines in the sand could be drawn or pawns taken or traded. There may have been, in Reaganesque soundbites, an Evil Empire, and Reagan may have had his own moments of autopilot if not incoherence, but the doctrine named after him depended on the Evil Empire responding and acting with an essential rationality.

If China and Vietnam were no longer a complication, Iran had been for Reagan's predecessor as president, Jimmy Carter. Although Carter had up till 1977 several times criticized the Shah of Iran for abuses of human rights, he spoke in support of the Shah when the latter was under severe pressure from public protests in the latter part of 1978, on the very eve of the Iranian revolution. After the success of the revolution, anger towards the US for its role in supporting the Shah lingered, and the seizing of hostages from the US embassy by the Tehran crowd was an expression of this. The hostage episode was a major embarrassment for the Carter administration, and a botched rescue mission only made things worse. It helped pave the way for Reagan's victory over Carter, and the new president was not going to risk any embarrassments by a direct confrontation with the new Iran. Besides, the idea of Islamic revolution was not something for which US policy makers were prepared. Washington think-tanks were by and large still devoted to Kremlin-watching rather than Koran-reading. It cannot be said that British experience in the Middle East would have been helpful either. Egypt's Nasser and the seizure of the Suez Canal had been aspects of a secular revolution. What was so pointedly, if self-declaredly, Islamic found no resonance in the rationalized world of US foreign policy. In a normal game the seizing of embassy hostages simply should not have taken place. Islam could not be said to be an aspect of the Soviet game plan either. Reagan left Iran out of direct US policy, but he did not ignore it completely. He was happily, if quietly, supportive of Saddam Hussein's invasion of Iran and the eight-year war that followed. Under those circumstances Iran would not be of significant bother to the West, and the West got on with its game with the Soviet Union and played for the Third World pawns who were not problematically Islamic and outside the calculations of the game.

Iran

This is not necessarily to speak approvingly of any of them, but there were three great revolutions in the twentieth century: in Russia, China and Iran. Even now the clumsy Western response to things Islamic is symptomatic of the surprise and lack of recognition as to its importance that greeted the Iranian revolution in 1979. The French philosopher Michel Foucault did recognize that something new was in the air. In a 1979 interview he spoke of the revolution as 'something quite different', as spirit in 'a world without spirit'. He said that many of his colleagues were waiting for an old-style, secular revolution to appear out of what manifestly had a spiritual content, but they would probably have to keep waiting. And even the secular revolutionaries in Tehran were themselves buoyed by the spirit, and the spiritual, of what had happened.

> At Tehran University, there were – I have met several of them – Marxists who were all conscious of living through a fantastic revolution. It was even much more than they had imagined, hoped for, dreamt about. Invariably, when asked what they thought, the Marxists replied: 'It's a revolutionary situation, but there's no vanguard.'[22]

The European left, themselves looking for a Leninist vanguard, also mistook the revolution. But the revolution was genuinely popular. It was also bloody, in that pogroms and revenge executions took place to purge public institutions and the armed forces of the Shah's supporters. But the first very few months were also times of cultural joy and expression. In the description of two writers who lived through the events, it was a 'Tehran Spring'. The revolution was officially won on 11 February 1979, but

> January to May 1979 saw the freest and culturally and politically most dynamic period of recent Iranian history. More than 250 publications flourished, including those of a wide spectrum of leftist and other secular factions, women's groups, regional tribal and ethnic groups, Jewish intellectuals and many other groupings. Magazines and journals banned under the Shah reappeared, and new ones were started. Book publishing enjoyed a heyday, with reissues of previously banned writers, great quantities of translation including large numbers of Marxist and leftist texts, religious pamphlets, and so forth. Cassette tapes of all kinds of music, but especially of revolutionary international songs and classical Persian music, were mass-produced.[23]

It took only a short time for this plurality and joy to pass. Factions within the revolution, united to depose the Shah, now fought each other. The result was a crushing victory for the clerical party of the Ayatollah Khomeini. However, despite the image of Khomeini as a fundamentalist devoid of Western influences, there was probably more to the man than this. Exiled for years in Paris, and in Iraq – where he was in contact with Palestinian intellectuals – he may have, and if not he then many of his followers, imbibed the sort of Third Worldism that arose from the legacy of Frantz Fanon and the neo-Marxist approach to dependency within the international political economy of the world.

> There is some convergence, not wholly accidental, between the 'Manichean' world outlook of Khomeini and other Muslim thinkers and the more widespread phenomenon of 'Third Worldism'. The Manichean trend sees the world as largely divided into the just Muslim oppressed and the Western or Western-tied oppressors, and the more general ideology of the Third World similarly sees itself as

economically drained and culturally colonized by an imperialist West.[24]

Of course, both 'Manichean' and Third World strands were hostile to the West – and we shall return to the 'Manichean' element later in this essay – but this observation does begin to multiply the reasons why the Iranian revolution could be forged by seemingly disparate partners. Even with the victory of the Khomeini faction, it was not as if all secular influences and virtues disappeared. One could still study Hegel and Kant at the University of Tehran, the Iranian diplomatic service fielded a stream of extraordinarily talented ambassadors whose cosmopolitan charms belied the hard edge of the Khomeini regime, and the Iranian constitution, meant to be an Islamic document, had to contain an array of clauses devoted to secular processes in a world that had to contain secular transactions, and other clauses to deal with the emergencies of modern life that had no precedent in *Sharia*.[25] Without this sort of intellectual and jurisprudential sociology, the reformers in today's power struggles in Tehran would have no platform. As it is, they stand on what may be tentative, at least implicit, strands and admissions that the clerical version of the revolution could not or would not abolish. Since many of the reformers are themselves clerics, the full intellectual history of the revolution will make fascinating reading when one day it is written.

None of this is to deny the ferocity and restrictiveness of the post-Tehran Spring revolution. And none of it dissuaded either the West or the Arab world from refusing to befriend Iran. Saddam Hussein, on 22 September 1980, began an eight-year war against Iran. It was a bitter and bloody war, fought to a stalemate, with perhaps a slight Iranian advantage at its end. Saddam conducted a pragmatic diplomacy with the Soviet Union, the US and the Arab world – the last anxious that popular revolutions should not multiply in its midst. In fact Saddam's relations with Washington improved remarkably in this period. Perhaps, in the muddled diplomatic signals that followed the end of the war with Iran, Saddam thought he had received Washington's sanction for his invasion of Kuwait: the Emirate as reward. But Saddam also forged close military relationships with France, the Soviet Union,

China and Egypt. The Arab world poured in US$60 billion to help Saddam fight his war.[26] Perhaps this helped the US to think there was no Islamic colossus in the future of international relations, and that the Iranian revolution – with its hardline Islamic turn – was only a blip at the end of a Cold War that had been fought with secular rationality, and the possibility of actual war planned for with even greater, purportedly 'scientific' rationality. The triumphalism that followed the West's victory at the end of the Cold War had no room within it for the possibility of gatecrashers at the party of celebration.

The end of history

When in 1990 Saddam Hussein marched into Kuwait he thought he had been given a subtle signal from the US that he had its permission. He would have had no intention of selling Kuwaiti oil to any other than its established customers in the West. The aim was to increase Iraqi revenue, not offend the West; it was also to increase Iraq's regional importance and, for that, he needed a good relationship with the US. But Saddam had misread the 'signal' he had received from the US ambassador to Iraq, or she had misread Saddam's solicitation of a signal and nodded for something quite other than the invasion of Kuwait. As it was, the US was very much not content with the idea that its oil-rich ally should be invaded by Iraq. Saddam may have had no intention of selling oil elsewhere than to the West and, indeed, no other mass market might have been possible, but the US, although happy to support him as an antagonist against Iran, was unhappy about a man with such obvious Iraqi as well as Iranian blood on his hands having any say on Kuwaiti oil flows.

In the first Gulf War that followed, from the end of 1990 into 1991, the US headed an immense coalition that included not only Britain and France (on British television, British soldiers led the way while, on French television, French soldiers did likewise – actually, it was probably the French who did the harder work) but units from several Islamic countries. The countries of the Middle East, although they too had been supportive of Saddam against Iran, were not keen on the precedent that he or anyone else should be able to march across a border. Today, Kuwait's border; would it be theirs tomorrow? Even so, huge protests against the US-led response to Saddam erupted throughout the Islamic world. As James Piscatori pointed out, these protests were in defence of Iraq as an Islamic country, despite Saddam's rule having been secular, but he did very quickly dress in the clothes of an Islamic martyr, although the protests arose from the people of countries with very many different brands of Islam.[27] Nevertheless the Western victory over Saddam allowed the first President Bush to declare the 'victory of liberalism'. By this he meant not just victory in the Gulf War but victory in the wake of the fall of Communism in 1989. The Cold War had been won in that symbolic moment when the Berlin Wall came down. Now, in the desert, Western values were deemed to have met their first post-Cold War test, and passed. And not only that but because most Islamic governments had rallied to the Western cause – never mind the protesting public in so many Islamic countries – it seemed that it was not merely Western liberalism that had won and was safe, but that its secular and rational nature had also won and was safe. Iran was exhausted and it seemed that the rest of the Islamic world was not going to do more than make noise, and the first President Bush seemed genuinely happy.

If this happiness had been expressed in no more than a few desert speeches and White House orations, the sense of a *fin de siècle* without foreboding – indeed with accomplished triumph ten years ahead of the millennium's turn – might not have been made to seem so strong. Washington, however, is a strangely intellectual town; that is, it gives a place to intellectual thought, and authors and pundits are always represented at black-tie functions. Perhaps more accurately, Washington gives a place to intellectual fashion, and the last 'designer thinker' had stirred at least polite apprehension that the US might not hold on to its pre-eminent global position as the twenty-first century advanced. Paul Kennedy's great book on the rise and fall of great powers seemed a studied warning not to take too much for granted. Watch out for the Chinese and Japanese, it seemed to say.[28] It was almost fitting, therefore, that the next great intellectual statement should come from a Japanese American, and that he should say that the US had not only done well, but that no one could do better.[29] The race had been won. History's purpose had been achieved. And this was said with enough philosophical apparatus (even if some of it seemed to come straight from his student notes[30]) to ensure its salon pedigree.

Francis Fukuyama's brief 1989 article, portentously (even if, as the question mark at the end suggested, nervously) entitled 'The End of History?', created a sensation of the sort impossible outside the US and France – an 'idea' dressed up for town and able to be marketed[31] – and this is also what happened to his follow-up book three years later.[32] And if no one noticed the question mark in the title of his article, few noticed the implication of the words at the end of the book title, 'the Last Man'. For Fukuyama had thought further since the idea came for his article. In that article he provided almost a *leitmotiv* for the triumphalism that followed the victories in the Cold and Gulf Wars. Following Hegel, history had ended with its own consummation, and liberal democracy had not only won but had established itself as the best possible government, as the best possible result of political history moving inexorably to this point. By the time of the book, Fukuyama had developed a more contingent view of this historical triumph. He elaborated the image of 'the last man', the person who inhabited the achievement of liberal history, but he warned also of the possibility of history restarting, and of a 'first man' of that new history.

Here Fukuyama mixed Hegel and Nietzsche – or at least the images they used – and suggested that the increasing comfort of 'last men' would produce 'men without chests', having desire and reason, but lacking *thymos* – the craving and demand for recognition. By contrast, the new 'first men', deprived and uncomfortable in the historically realized world, would not exhibit the historically conditioned and civilized attributes of desire and reason – they would thereby be 'bestial' – but be consumed by *thymos* alone. In their desire for recognition the slaves would rise against the masters and restart history.

Perhaps Fukuyama should be seen as prophetic, but some few years later no one called Osama Bin Laden the 'first man', though bestial adjectives were certainly used. Instead, if there was such a thing as a 'last man', he took himself seriously and considered digging the bunkers, drawing the boundary lines and manning the watchtowers of the world where history required no further development. The only problem was that the US had never realized how impossibly 'un-Western' so much of the West actually could be. I shall return to this point later. For now, the end of the Cold War meant the sudden enlargement of 'Europe'. It was no longer simply Western Europe but a difficult amalgam of Eastern and Western, and the Western side was determined that the Eastern should once again imbibe those Enlightenment values that Communism had, after all, only briefly interrupted. This, however, proved a very difficult project indeed.[33]

Dogs in the manger

One of the anomalies of the Cold War was Tito's Yugoslavia. A composite country under a federal structure, it was meant to be a success story of supernational as opposed to petty nationalism. Its former, ever contentious, component parts had played a role in twentieth-century European history. Sarajevo had after all been the flashpoint of the First World War. Woodrow Wilson's entire post-war project of open diplomacy was to avoid the secret dealings and treaties that had sucked Europe into that conflict. In the Second World War, Tito's partisans tied down far more German divisions than their motley strength would have suggested. Allied, particularly British, advisers worked secretly with them. Major Frank Thompson, brother of the British historian and campaigner, E.P. Thompson, was executed with many of them by the fascist authorities, and this sort of cooperation and sacrifice helped lay down an enduring affection between the British left and Yugoslavia. More to the point, Yugoslavia's participation in the Cold War was a masterpiece of deliberately anomalous policy and diplomacy. For the European left, Tito's version of socialism was camped somewhere between social democracy and Communism proper. For the West as a whole, Yugoslavia retained sufficient financial and economic structures compatible with those of the Western bloc for the country to be made the only associate member of the OECD (Organization for Economic Cooperation and Development), which harmonized the economic policies of the great capitalist powers in the world. And for the globally emerging Third World Tito played a significant role in founding the Non-Aligned Movement – the worthy but futile effort to stand equidistant to the two feuding super-powers. Global, Western and European, Yugoslavia had cultural habits that were firmly those of Europe. Even when it was most officially Communist, it remained an historically isolated but curious replica of what the Habsburg Empire and its social values had been. The French intellectual Alain Finkielkraut, writing to protest against the Serbian atrocities of the 1990s, declared each of Yugoslavia's successor nations – especially Croatia and Bosnia – to be in some way European. That is, not East European, nor queuing for admission to Europe, but nations in which Europe should be interested precisely because they were European.[34] If, in the triumph of liberal democracy after the Cold War, the West could not absorb Yugoslavia and its successor states, then what could it absorb?

The tensions and fault-lines in the Yugoslavian experiment were, however, long apparent.[35] The country has re-split into its component parts: Slovenia (now within the European Union), Croatia, Serbia (with its now tangential link with Montenegro), Kosovo (still laid claim to by Serbia),[36] and Macedonia (as much bandit and warlord territory as republic). But Alexander the Great came from Macedonia and carried the early Western legacy eastwards. To consider these parts of Europe to be too violent and problematic to be part of the future Western project would be embarrassingly to deny some important history. And yet the decade of bloodshed immediately after the Cold War, and its seeming intractability – the fighting and slaughters at Vukovar and Srebrenica, the endless siege of Sarajevo, once a European City of Culture – coming only to a spluttering halt with massive Western intervention, the bombing of Belgrade and the war crimes tribunal in The Hague, all seemed to suggest something outside the Western project. Here was *thymos* alone, but where was reason and civilized desire? And why was it, some-how mixed up in it all, that an Islamic issue arose? In what ways were the Bosnians Muslim? Is that why the Serbs fought them? Some age-old religious divide? And what were all these stories of Iranian fighters coming to help the Bosnians defend their terri-tory? Never mind that the Iranian volunteers ended up as bemused as the Nigerian UN peacekeeping soldiers standing guard in a Balkan winter. Even if unsuccessful, what sort of solidarity was this?

To these questions were added others that had long been apparent during the Cold War, but which now had added impetus. If the victors of the Cold War had accomplished something globally historical, if liberal democracy and its values had triumphed, why was there still a running sore in the Middle East over Israel? And why, despite being themselves at least originally Semitic, did Israel seem besieged on all sides by those who were differentiated from them as Arab states, not as other Semitic nations? What was the quality of being Arab? And what was the quality of being Israeli? Is there a serious question that hinges on Israel, and no other Middle Eastern nation, being invited to compete in the Eurovision Song Contest? And, if its only victor in that contest was a transsexual vamp, can her nation also cross boundaries, or have those been cemented by recent European atrocity upon the reconstruction of an historical space? Certainly that sense of space, and its ownership, has been writ large in the notion of an *Eretz* or Biblical Israel, stretching somewhat further than the state's present, even controversially enlarged, borders. Some enthusiastic writers have even suggested right of occupation by virtue of no other habitation at the time of the modern state's foundation, i.e. that no Palestinians actually lived there.[37] What I want to suggest here, however, is the incorporation of a European identity into that which proposes now to be Jewish. It is this that incorporates Israel into the West.

The fact of the Holocaust having taken place in Europe, and the bulk of the six million killed having been European Jews, has meant a tremendous identification with the new homeland on the part of European Jewry and their American cousins of European descent. The books by Primo Levi narrating the terrible sufferings and bids for survival are all populated by Europeans, jealous of their culture and refined in what can only be described as their European sensibilities. In one book Levi recounts the words not of a concentration camp inmate but one of the rare Jewish resistance fighters:

We want to fight the Germans till the end of the war, and – who knows? – maybe even afterwards. Then we'll try to go away. We want to go to Palestine; in Europe there's no place for us anymore. Hitler's won the war against the Jews, and even his pupils have done a good job. Everybody has learned his gospel: Russians, Lithuanians, Croats, Slovaks. ... Dov spoke up ... we fought as Russians first and as Jews second.[38]

When Palestine, later Israel, was just a dream, the European Jews were as European as they were Jewish. And, of those who did stay in Europe, there are no end of examples of European sensibility: Isaiah Berlin comes to mind with his love of Russian thinkers and German composers. And as for those who did go to the new Israel, and had to fight again, their successful military campaigns were inspired by British strategists such as Fuller and Liddell Hart and, ironically, the German Panzer general, Guderian.

Even when someone like Egypt's President Sadat had in his negotiating entourage brilliant US PhD-trained advisers and ministers, it was never quite enough. Perhaps, in the account by Sydney Bailey, it was as Kissinger said, 'I admit I am afraid of Arab romanticism'[39] – although this romanticism may be a direct product of the way the language is constructed. In any case, as Bailey went on to observe, it was the Arabs who had preserved Greek culture during Europe's dark ages. Not that this meant very much to Kissinger, whose own view of how to structure a peaceful world was based on his appreciation of how Europe was brought together again after the conquering and constitutional adventures of Napoleon.[40] There are Europes and Europes, and the Europe of today's international policies, and the US that is only recently descended from Europe, are pretty modern footsteps in history. The West that they claim to represent can shrink still further. There may be yet what the Afrikaner defenders of apartheid called a *laager* mentality – the drawing of wagons into a defensible circle. And it is clear that events in the Balkans and Palestine, with an Islamic element in each, and with a larger Islamic storm seeming to be brewing particularly over the latter, caused many US thinkers and policy makers to rethink the boundaries of what it was the US and West should defend.

So that on Samuel Huntington's controversial but revealing map of 'The World of Civilizations, Post 1990',[41] South Africa is

not part of the West (despite decades of US effort to regard it as
so), nor is Mexico (despite the North American Free Trade
Association), but nor are Greece and Israel. Malaysia, Singapore,
Papua New Guinea, the Falkland Islands and French Guiana are.
Croatia and Slovenia are, but the rest of former Yugoslavia is not.
Lithuania, Latvia and Estonia are – basically all those that are
members or are likely to seek membership of the European
Union, with the exception of Greece which is both a member of
the EU and NATO and gave rise to Western civilization. Turkey,
a member of NATO, is also not part of the West.

What Huntington has done is to have divided his world into
a number of confessional zones. The problematically non-
Western Greece and former Yugoslavia are 'Orthodox', along
with Russia, although how Catholicism (Croatia) is more Western than Orthodoxy (Serbia) is not easily explained. Nor are the
different types of Orthodoxy – Greek Orthodoxy being a case
much to itself, and, of course, there is a great deal of Orthodoxy
within the West, particularly within Germany and Holland. Still,
the Huntington thesis requires borderlands. It is an old-
fashioned geopolitics dressed in the cloth of ideas – but geopolitics requires geographical boundaries. Along with the Orthodox,
also camped near the borders of the 'West' is a swathe called
'Islamic'.

This sort of thinking is not new in the US. Thomas Sowell
published a book, shortly before Huntington's, in which he
advocated the use of 'cultural capital' as a foundation for pros-
perity[42] – e.g. Chinese people work hard – and a species of what
is properly a cultural essentialism may of course be used to differ-
entiate, divide, draw lines between the peoples of the world.
Edward Said has recently identified those who influenced the
White House in its contemporary cultural essentialism towards
the Middle East – Bernard Lewis and Fouad Ajami, who spoke of
an 'Arab mind', and of a centuries-old Arab decline which only
the US (on its own terms of course) could reverse.[43] I want to
return to this later. In the meantime each 'civilization' could fit
neatly into one space, and each space is neatly held as a set of
cultural ideas and values.

Huntington's book, like Fukuyama's before him, was an attempt to flesh out a bright idea in a short article,[44] and the basic idea that required fleshing was that the US and the West, with deeply held core values, were threatened by other societies with equally deeply held core values. That these were therefore different, if not opposing, 'civilizations' was the source of Edward Said's complaint that Huntington had made a significant mistake in basic definitions.[45] Nothing, as Said wrote, is as isolated and insulated as a 'civilization' must be in Huntington's terms. There is, for instance, as Akbar Ahmed pointed out, plenty of post-modernism in Islam as well,[46] not to mention albums in the West released by members of the Rolling Stones and Led Zeppelin with Islamic musicians from different North African countries. The response to Huntington by the Iranian scholar Kaveh Afra-siabi was particularly telling: criticizing Huntington from a wide range of modern *Western* philosophical sources, and demonstrating that Huntington had finally rejected the universalism that was at the core of the West's Enlightenment. What was even more interesting was that Afrasiabi's brief article to this effect in a Western journal,[47] was only a version of an article he published in Iran, in which he indulged himself by citing a massive array of Western authors, from Arnold Toynbee and Joseph Needham to Michel Foucault and Jürgen Habermas.[48] There are more West-ern writers cited in this article than there are Islamic writers cited in the 12 chapters of Huntington's book.

It is easy to fall into point-scoring here.[49] What is important is two-fold. Firstly, you had better have a discerning and accurate historical base for your definitions; and, secondly and more importantly, if the global choice is to divide and defend, or expand and embrace, why not do the latter? But, if the latter, who is it who expands and who is it who embraces whom on whose terms? Did anyone ever trust a lover who came with a gun? The US in particular has been torn between the two, and when it has sought to pay courtship to the world the gun has been hol-stered over its heart.

Not that the US actually thought it would do this. When the second George Bush took office everyone believed in the possi-bility of a new US isolationism - not as rigorous as that before the Second World War and the Cold War, but non-interventionist and self-concerned. Moreover, and this is a problem that has bedevilled everything since: whenever the military tried to model a war between the US and an enemy *without* a discrete space of its own, a territory, preferably for consequential legal and diplomatic reasons a state, it did not know how to do it. If there were inklings within the new US administration of a stateless, no-fixed-base, no-standing-army threat, these were not allowed to develop. To be fair, the new president had a terrible learning curve. After all, he was the candidate who when asked for his opinion on the Taliban thought it was a heavy-metal rock group. At least, as he quickly learned, the Taliban did inhabit a geopolitical space. Many international fighters, of varying moral stripe, had also come to live in that space.

For the self-enclosed world of US military planners all geographical space had to become a form of political space – each space had a political value – and all spaces and all values could be modelled. This is why Huntington's book was well received in Washington. This was the common way of thinking, even if its more arcane methodologies were secret. The arcania had nevertheless to be programmable into the Pentagon's computers. All space and its values finally became programmable into cyberspace, and all wars in the foreseeable future had already been modelled, rehearsed (and won) in this cyberspace.[50] The US was as ready for anything as it could be. There was both this readiness, and a feeling that the US might be well advised to retreat to safer borders in the Huntington mode, leaving only Israel as an outpost of Europe and the West – problem strewn, ill fitting but fully admitted. It was then that September 11 arrived out of the sky.

2 THE FIRST MAN AND THE STUDENTS OF GOD

From their Saracen opponents in the Middle East the Christian Crusaders learnt many things: a greater appreciation of medicine and mathematics, and the code of chivalry in which a woman, for the first time in medieval Europe, could be treated as a creature with individual metaphysical complexities and personality, and be loved and championed for them. Without this contact, King Arthur would have remained in legend as a gruff post-Roman or Breton warlord, and Gawain would not have been famed for his 'seemliest manners and ... faultless figures of virtuous discourse. ... This noble knight will prove what manners the mighty bring; his converse of courtly love shall spur our studying.'[1] If anything refined the Europe of that time it was the young Islam. There is a wonderful story of a meeting between Richard the Lionheart and the Saracen Sultan, Saladin. It was during a truce and Richard strode into Saladin's tent, took out his great broadsword and swung it down on a log being readied for the fireplace. The log was chopped asunder and Richard beamed, 'This is the sword of England!' Saladin, quite unfazed, picked up a square of silk, tossed it in the air, drew his scimitar and razor-sliced it in two. 'This,' he said, 'is the sword of Islam.' What was a test of swords could also have been a test of thought but, to be fair, this would have been with an Islam at its intellectual height. Its debates were infused with neo-Aristotelian and neo-Platonic thought – what the Sufi poet Attar called 'the thought of Alexander'.[2] Hundreds of years after the test of swords, Gustave Doré published an impressive engraving of Saladin triumphant in battle. It was Richard who was defeated. Saladin is armoured and his flowing cape merges into the flowing mane and tail of his horse. He could be St George but, instead of a cross on his helmet, he wears a crescent. It was a rare moment of Western generosity of image towards the Muslim world and one of its great heroes.

Yet that Muslim world has somehow been long generous to the West and its heroes. Not only Greek thought but the compassionate figure of Christ was given much portrayal in early Islamic literature. An excerpt from one ninth-century portrait will suffice here:

> Christ passed by a group of Israelites who insulted him. Every time they spoke a word of evil, Christ answered with good. Simon the pure said to him, 'Will you answer them with good each time they speak evil?' Christ said, 'Each person spends of what he owns.'[3]

Perhaps this is as true of a 'civilization' as a person; yet, 1,000 years after these words of Christ recounted by a Muslim author, figures from both the Christian and Muslim worlds brand the other as 'evil'. After 9/11 the most 'evil' man on earth, certainly from the US perspective, was Osama Bin Laden, then resident in Afghanistan. But, when Osama was on the run, first from the Russians then from US forces, he tended to travel with a huge library. Visitors to his mountain cave would enter the library first – by that I mean an antechamber with tall bookshelves – and the living quarters next. In fact this sort of 'refugee in the mountains' establishment was not uncommon. Osama's principal Afghan enemy (until Osama had him assassinated on the eve of 9/11), Ahmed Shah Massoud, travelled with a library of 3,000 books (and wore Gucci boots under his traditional *shalwar kameez*). It was Massoud's poster-size photograph that adorned many Northern Alliance vehicles as they were driven into Kabul when the Taliban fell. A darling of Western intellectuals, Massoud may have had books by the French thinker Bernard-Henri Levy in his library, if only because Levy, unctuous always on his own behalf, would have gifted them on his visits to Massoud. Perhaps Osama retained some of the textbooks for his US-curriculum MBA in his library – perhaps a souvenir programme from his boyhood visit to Disneyland? Or, if they were all books on Islamic themes, does it take thousands of books to make a 'fundamentalist'? Did Massoud and Osama have the same Islamic titles on their different shelves – carried by their different donkeys on their various flights? How did the same books make an 'intellectual fighter in the Byronic mould' out of one, and a 'fundamentalist Muslim purveyor of evil and murder' out of the other? The problem is: if you take the Fukuyama/Nietzschean image of the First Man Restarting History, you can't just say that someone like Osama was driven by *thymos* alone. There was desire and reason there, probably a lot of reason, but the avalanche of 'evil' in our labelling has buried this, and we shall never know his reasons for 9/11 until we ourselves begin to excavate the Ground Zero of our hatred.

Afghanistan

Afghanistan was always something of a crossroads, a melting pot of Indian, Persian, Transcaucasian and Chinese influences. It was a perfect transit route for the spread of Buddhism northwards from India. Buddhism didn't get waylaid, enclosed by mountains and superimposed upon local gods, as in Tibet. Afghanistan monumentalized some parts of it, as in the huge rock-cut Buddhas at Bamiyan (which the Taliban later destroyed), made fluid and florid other parts (as in its sensuous statues of Bodhisattvas or saints) by using plaster techniques (if not plaster) imported from Alexandria in Egypt, and made Western the rest. The famous Gandharan sculptures of northern India, where Buddha appears almost like a young Greek warrior, were apparent also in Afghanistan where the imported Hellene sculptors had to pass. Afghanistan put Buddhism into a melting pot of cosmopolitan influences before sending it on to China. Probably most importantly, Persian or Iranian ideas from Zoroastrianism infiltrated Buddhism via Afghanistan. Indian Buddhism tells of Buddha overcoming evil, of being able to exit the world of *samsara*. Zoroastrianism, though an advocate of monotheism, establishes a dualism of good and evil, through which the human journey must navigate. If there is one thing Nietzsche got right in his portentous adaptation of the Zoroastrian story, in *Thus Spake Zarathustra* (and inspiring the even more dreadfully portentous overture from Strauss, or what most of us know as the theme from *2001: A Space Odyssey*), it is that the navigation is hard.

In fact forms of Manicheanism flourished in Afghanistan. Alexander and his armies came and went – though much Greek influence stayed – and, as time passed, Arab armies came and

went leaving Islam in their wake. At the time of the first millennium, the huge Iranian renaissance in art and literature swept
through Afghanistan also. In the thirteenth century Genghis
Khan also swept through, although he left no cultural renaissance in his wake. (His soldiers left a pretty strong ethnic imprint
upon Iran, however.) In the fourteenth century, Taimur, or
Tamburlaine in Christopher Marlowe's play, also conquered
Afghanistan. Marlowe has Tamburlaine soliloquizing to his
lieutenants on the anticipated joys of being a king – 'to be a king
... and march in triumph through Persepolis' – but if that Mongol prince never did quite make it to Iranian triumph his son
established his own capital in Herat, Afghanistan, and invited
Iranian culture to come to it. Later visitors would say, 'the whole
habitable world had not such a town as Herat'. The years that
followed saw much two-way traffic. Afghan forces would annex
huge tracts of India – even taking and ruling from Delhi. Within
Afghanistan itself, the different tribal or national groups would
also fight and endlessly redraw territorial maps, but outside
players were never far from the scene, and the modern story must
really begin in the nineteenth century with the 'Great Game'
between Russia and Britain for control of Afghanistan as the
entry point to India.

In a sense, nothing much has changed for Afghanistan. It has
had a history of upheaval and instability, splendour with different cultural influences, quarrels and war, an endless stream of
prophets and sages in its mountains (Gjurdief being one of the
more recent), armies sweeping through, rulers and resistance
leaders packing books into their mountain retreats. Fighting on
the run had a slightly different meaning to that in the West.
What has changed is the external image of the country. No one
speaks any more like the astonished visitor to Herat (which once
had its own warrior queen). The image is of a backward and
parochial, quarrelsome, tribalized, treacherous and conservative
society, presided over by greedy and bloody warlords. Perhaps it
is a true image, on the surface. It was an image the British had,
but it is well to remember that the (somewhat noble) 'border
thief', Kamal, in Rudyard Kipling's famous poem, 'The Ballad of
East and West 1889', was an Afghan warlord. Kipling is mostly

depicted by today's post-colonial scholars as an imperial apologist. This is not fully correct and is lazily one-dimensional. This particular poem, after all, celebrates an essential equality between a jesting and dashing young son of an English colonel, and an Afghan 'border thief'. Not that Kamal was called Afghan: in the nineteenth-century contest for borders all tribesmen in the region were simply Pashtun. But the poem's refrain, usually truncated to the negative opening line that East and West will never meet, in fact ends on the most positive note: 'But there is neither East nor West, Border, nor Breed, nor Birth, When two strong men stand face to face, though they come from the ends of the earth!' The interesting thing is that the colonel's son and Kamal never actually test their strength against each other. They recognize their fundamental equality in the qualities of daring and honour. These two qualities also have been read out of today's image of Afghanistan.

If the British eventually gave up their need for the Khyber Pass, disbanded their Bengal Lancers and ended what had been the greatest foreign game of Victoria's era, the Russians never quite withdrew their interest in the region. We remember today the splash they made in 1979 when, 'out of a blue sky' – without warning, signal or detectable build-up – the Soviet military machine marched into Afghanistan and established what seemed a puppet government in Kabul. If the West was astonished, its pride wounded that its intelligence services had not seen it coming, it was the Chinese who were devastated. For half a dozen years they had been patiently proselytizing a Three-World Theory, in which China led the Third World and defended it. Unable even to contemplate the defence of Kabul, the Chinese finally abandoned any aspiration towards an overarching world policy and philosophy, and the Soviets had completed what Kissinger and Nixon had begun.[4] But had the Soviets simply marched in? This is the moment to add detail to the recent history of a grand, seemingly surreal tapestry of a land.

A twentieth-century history[5]

Modern Afghanistan is said to begin at the end of the nineteenth century with the British installation of Abdor Khan as head of a central government. What this did was not so much to create a puppet, but a strong-enough governing force to make Afghanistan a credible buffer state between British interests in India and the Russian Empire. The borders drawn from that period reflect the role of Afghanistan. Both Abdor Khan and his successor, Habibollah Khan, strove to reform their country. Every time they liberalized their rule, however, faction-fighting reappeared, so that in 1919 Habibollah was assassinated and Amanollah Khan assumed power. He promptly engaged in a minor war with the British, recognized the new Bolshevik government in Moscow, sought to introduce some socialist ideas and the secularism of Atatürk's Turkey, and demanded that the *Loya Jirga*, the Great Council of tribal chiefs, dress in Western clothes. Hereditary titles were to be abolished, there was to be a parliament, and all literate men were to have the vote. The women's veil was to be abolished and schools were to become co-educational. Amanollah was promptly overthrown. Governments briefly came and went thereafter but that of Mohammed Zahir Shah lasted 30 years till 1973. Shah tried to keep equidistance between the two great superpowers but, by the time of the 1970s, he was reliant on Soviet aid to develop his country. The British had long left the scene, but the Russians had not.

Under King Zahir Shah, the prime minister, Mohammed Daud, cultivated the Soviets. Arguments with Pakistan over the status of the Pashtun tribe who lived on either side of the border meant the closure of that border in 1961. The border with the Soviet Union thus provided the only remaining trade route. In the context of reliance on the Soviet Union and the failure of the king's efforts at reform, Daud seized power in 1973, overthrew the monarchy and declared a republic. He did this in concert with the local Communist party (in which, to be fair, Moscow had taken almost no interest – it was as home-grown as it could be) and two other ambitious faction-leaders, Babrak Karmal and Nur Mohammed Taraki. It was an uneasy tribal alliance and, in the weight/counterweight manoeuvres that followed, the local Communists grew in power. They overthrew Daud in 1978 and installed Taraki. Babrak Karmal was made deputy prime minister. Taraki's efforts at reform were met with tremendous tribal and conservative resistance. Crisis followed crisis in a very short time. Taraki died under mysterious circumstances in September 1979, his brief successor was killed in December 1979, and Babrak Karmal - who had been exiled in one of the power struggles - returned to head the state. Simultaneously, whether at Karmal's invitation or independently, and alarmed by the situation on its frontiers, the Soviets sent in 80,000 troops. They stayed to support first Karmal, then his successor in 1981, Sayid Mohammed Najibullah. It was at this point that the already woeful history of Afghanistan became compounded.

Najibullah went out of his way to bring the Mujaheddin, the tribally based leaders and their followers, into line if not into alliance. He created a new constitution and a formal legislature, legalized political parties, and appointed to senior positions people not sympathetic to him. He sought to have as much of this as possible discussed in and ratified by various efforts at tribal assemblies. Even when, as late as April 1988, the Mujaheddin boycotted elections to the National Assembly, Najibullah left 50 seats vacant for them.

None of this is to say that Najibullah was a good leader or a good man. He manoeuvred as well (or as dirtily) as any in Afghan politics. However, it was his reforms that alienated the Mujaheddin. Under them, the country was not going to modernize. They would rather go to war than give up their own power or change their political ways and social customs. But they commanded great loyalty. Thousands of soldiers deserted to join the Mujaheddin, bringing their Soviet armaments with them. Low-intensity rebellion flared into serious war by 1985. At this stage, large quantities of Chinese and particularly American arms began to be delivered to the Mujaheddin, usually via Pakistan. Above all, the US provided surface-to-air missiles, which shot down a huge number of Soviet helicopters and gunships. The Soviets, embittered by the futility of trying to make Afghanistan work, and counting their rising losses, had withdrawn by February 1989 - their ten-year intervention a complete disaster. By 1991 the US had also realized that it was impossible to persuade the various factions to cooperate with one another, and cut back on its military aid. By that time, the Mujaheddin had quite enough hardware to overthrow Najibullah, which it did in 1992.

This triggered two years of incessant inter-factional struggle. Kabul was devastated repeatedly by artillery attacks and counter-attacks. Nor was the countryside at peace, as the power struggle affected all corners of life, and, as usual in such circumstances, depradations, corruptions, depravities and excesses multiplied themselves upon the common people. The US had empowered one monster to defeat another, and now the newly empowered monster was out of control. It was in these circumstances that a Robin Hood figure arose.

A late twentieth-century romance spawns a tragedy

In the spring of 1994 Mullah Mohammed Omar, a poor cleric and schoolmaster in a rural village, at the age of 35 – having been blinded in his right eye (one of four wounds) fighting against Najibullah – received a delegation of neighbours. They told him that a local Mujaheddin military commander had kidnapped two teenaged girls, cut off their hair and had handed them over to his garrison where they were repeatedly raped. Omar was outraged. He gathered 30 *talibs*, theology students from the local *madrassas* or private seminaries – usually the only source of education available – and found 16 rifles. With these 16 rifles they stormed the base, freed the girls and hung the commander from the gun barrel of one of his own tanks. A few months later Omar re-peated this sort of rescue, this time saving a young boy whom two commanders had been seeking to sodomize. Word spread quickly, and the legend of Omar was made. So was the legend of the theology students – more accurately 'the Students of God' – who helped him. Collectively they were the *taliban*, and a move-ment against corruption and misuse of power was born.[6]

Within two years the Taliban had swept all southern and eastern Afghanistan and were laying bloody siege to Kabul. Their successes were due as much to military inexperience as prowess. Not aware of conventions and precautions, such as regrouping after a victory, they ploughed on from one victory to the next, their supply lines outrageously slender or non-existent. They amassed much war material very quickly, some of it facilitated by Pakistan, but became renowned for not knowing how to use or deploy it properly. Their field command structure was either chaotic or non-existent. Omar would send out orders on the back of cigarette packets. By rights they should have won nothing, but they were now several tens of thousand strong – their numbers swollen by students from the Pakistani madrassas – and they were rigidly, inflexibly incorrupt. It may rightly or wrongly be called fundamentalism, but it was also idealism – setting out to rid an entire country of endless years of unholy rule.

Particularly in the south, popular support rallied behind the Taliban. Through it all, Omar's reputation held the movement together. In April 1996 he consolidated all the southern leaders behind him by an act of the most audacious (if he had failed to pull it off, it would have been said to have been blasphemous) imagination. At a convention of those leaders, amidst disgruntlement over the Taliban's failure to take Kabul, and rivalries beginning to eye the strength of his position, Omar marched to the shrine in Kandahar, found one of Islam's holiest relics – the cloak of Mohammed the Prophet – wrapped it around him, then went to the roof of a tall building in the city centre. Everyone could see what was floating in the wind around his shoulders. He declared himself 'Commander of the Faithful'. It also meant Emir of Afghanistan. Some took the action also to mean 'Heir to Mohammed'. For months, during the US-led war in Afghanistan, TV images replayed a clip of Omar putting on this cloak. It was the only footage of him that existed. Not a single commentator paused to say what was going on, or what the significance of the swirling cloak around his shoulders was. But in the Old Testament when Elijah is transported to heaven by God's chariot, he throws his cloak to Elisha who is standing awestruck down below. It was the sign of succession.

The previously stalled siege of Kabul was renewed with vigour. The Taliban were much given to frontal assaults, but their poor efforts at coordination – and hence concentration of armour in one place – meant that the defender of Kabul, Ahmed Shah Massoud, was able to break up the Taliban formations before they could build up critical steam. Commanding a force of only 25,000 men, Massoud fought a brilliant defence against an enemy that was by now much larger. But, with only 25,000 men, Massoud could not counterattack. He could only hold a line, and only hold it in one place at a time.

The Taliban did not give up their love for frontal assaults. What they did was to stage lightning strikes to take the provinces surrounding Kabul. Again, without pausing for breath or re-supply, they breathlessly seized all strategic points leading to Kabul. In some ways it was a masterpiece of mobile warfare. The advent of the Toyota four-wheel-drive pickup has still not been recognized in the West as the single greatest innovation in Third World wars. From the plains of Chad to the streets of Mogadishu and to the hills of Afghanistan, the machine-gun-mounted Toyotas have become the cavalry of the century's end and the millennium's beginning. Massoud recognized what the Taliban were about to attempt: not one frontal assault, but four simultaneously, from four different directions. Massoud could not deploy his slender resources to face four attacks at once, and he withdrew from Kabul. The Taliban were ever after to say that the city fell without a shot being fired on 26 September 1996, but Massoud wanted to husband his resources and regroup. He held the north and would have won another day if a certain Osama Bin Laden, guest-fighter with the Mujaheddin and supporter of the Taliban, had not assassinated him two days before 9/11.

Massoud attempted one last act of chivalry before the fall. The former Soviet-backed president, Najibullah, had sought and found sanctuary in a UN compound and had lived there since his fall. Too proud to leave Kabul, he now found himself deserted by UN personnel who had all fled. Massoud offered Najibullah safe escort with his own forces out of Kabul, but Najibullah was too proud, as a southerner, to accept the offer of a northern warrior. He refused and awaited his fate. That fate, at the hands of the Taliban, was to be beaten, castrated, further tortured, then hanged from a lamppost in a public street. There was to be no mercy in the strict rule of the Students of God.

If a mere five years later, when the US was imposing a new president in Afghanistan, Massoud had still been alive, maybe the country would have pulled behind his leadership more coherently than that of the current president. But Massoud was a northerner and a warlord, and, if there is one thing worse than a warrior warlord, it is a bookish intellectual warlord. He probably would not have been chosen. Perhaps he would have refused. In

any case he had been no saint and had enough treacheries and
bloodshed on his hands to fill a philosophy book or two. And, as
the US found, if there is one thing worse than an international
terrorist, it is a bookish intellectual terrorist who had cut his
fighting teeth waging war against the Soviets, hand-to-hand it
should be said, who had turned his back on his palace-brat
upbringing and devoted his share of the family fortune to building schools and hospitals in an alien land and preparing to wage
war on the West. If there was something apocalyptic about
Osama, it was also because he wished to seem so.

Osama

Standing 6'5", with his long robes and long beard, Osama Bin
Laden is either impossibly handsome (he is a poster-hero in
Pakistan and the Middle East, just as Che Guevara was in the
West) or implacably sinister. He based himself in northern
Pakistan from 1980, using his money to build much infrastructure for the Mujaheddin, and himself crossing the border
frequently to take part in the fighting. He was wounded several
times and, apparently, had had enough close escapes to consider
himself living on borrowed time. By rights he should already be
dead but, somehow – 'perhaps Allah protected him' – he always
survived. The failure of US troops to capture him has only added
to his mystique. Back in 1980, however, the international bri-
gades flocking to Afghanistan – including the so-called 'Arab
Afghans', the Saudi contingent of which was led by Osama – saw
the war against the Soviet occupiers as a *jihad*, as fighting for a
holy cause. To these veterans of the Afghan campaign, the withdrawal of Soviet forces in February 1989 was a direct precursor of
the fall of Communism later that year in Europe. When, later, it
came to war against the US it was thought that if one superpower
could be defeated why not another?

In 1990 Osama returned to Saudi Arabia, but not before
establishing in 1989 an organization called *Al Qaeda*, 'the Military Base', which was meant to be a coordinating group for all
the various 'Arab Afghans' who had come to fight, and to look
after their families. At the time there was nothing more sinister
about Al Qaeda than that, except that the Arab Afghans had
been kept at arm's length by their host Afghans. The foreign

fighters espoused too pure and too strict an Islam for the Mujaheddin. They, and Osama himself, were seen as self-righteous, as
coming from richer countries, and as looking beyond the rela-
tively backward Afghan fighters and their local cause. Osama was
restless in Saudi Arabia. He went to fight in Sudan, and there
found many fellow-thinkers who, like him, were disgruntled by
the US victory in the first Gulf War and the triumphalism that
followed. Osama assembled the leaders of international fighters
and took them back with him to Afghanistan in 1996 – finding
the Taliban as pure and as strict as himself – and began issuing
fatwas and announcing a *jihad* against the US. In 1997 he moved
to Jalalabad, not far from Mullah Omar, and the two became
friends. If there was one person who influenced the idealistic but
narrow-minded cleric, it was Osama. He filled Omar's mind with
a vision of an international fight far beyond the mountain borders of one country. The US responded by despatching a crack
CIA snatch-squad to Pakistan in February 1997. Its aim was to
abduct Osama from Afghanistan, but it failed. Osama's Al Qaeda
blew up the US embassies in Dar es Salaam and Nairobi in 1998,
and in November 1998 the US declared a $5 million price on his
head. In effect, today's great game between Osama and the US
began in 1998.

Today that great game continues. On 7 October 2001 Osama
broadcast a defiant message on Al Jazeera: 'Hypocrisy stood
behind the leader of global idolatry – behind the Hubal of the
age – namely, America and its supporters.'[7] This was a broadcast
to rally international Islamic support. The keyword here is 'Hubal'. When Abraham became a worshipper of the One True
God, i.e. when he embraced monotheism, when he embraced
Allah, he built a shrine in honour of God. This was in Mecca.
After the Arab tribes fell away from God it took many centuries
before Mohammed began preaching his Oneness again. In that
time, in what is now Islam's holiest shrine – the shrine conse-
crated by Abraham – the fallen Arabs had installed an idol,
Hubal. Mohammed, of course, wiped Hubal away.

Osama's broadcast had two levels of interpretation, both
directed against the US. On the wider level, it was a critique of
the US lifestyle that was being exported internationally: shallow,

materialistic and commodified; it was a lifestyle of idolatry, the worship of things. On the more specific level, since Hubal sat in Mecca, it was a critique of US military bases in Saudi Arabia. If Osama had an internationalist agenda, he had also a desire to rid Arabia of the House of Saud and its reliance on the US. Two years later the US would announce a withdrawal programme from Saudi Arabia – the Saudis knowing just how many chords Osama had touched – but only because it could now forward-base in Iraq, conquered after the second Gulf War.

The corruption of the House of Saud, however, had been formative for the young Osama. He embraced an austere Wahhabism, what seemed to be a desert-Spartan sect of strict – what many would call fundamentalist – Islam. There are some who see parallels between Osama's Wahhabism and Qaddafi's Sanusi background, but King Idris before Qaddafi was also Sanusi, and Qaddafi has frequently declared Arabism to be the stronger organizing principle over and above Islam.[8] For Osama, it was Islam that had political as well as religious priority. What was indeed an immediate parallel was that between Osama's Wahhabism and the fundamentalist teachings of the northern Pakistani and southern Afghan madrassas – what has been called Deobandism.

Deobandism was founded in what is now Pakistan as an organizational and ideological means of resisting British colonial rule. It remained after independence, if only because its madrassas, part-schools and part-seminaries, were the only means of education in northern Pakistan. As Pakistani governments serially became corrupt and inept, and as state education for both these reasons never penetrated the north to any degree, the madrassas grew. As they grew, the northern borderlands, as they had been in British times, became off-limits to official administration. By the end of the Cold War there were 8,000 registered madrassas and 25,000 unofficial ones. Many of these were run by clerics who were themselves only sketchily educated, and it is fair to say that the original Deobandism was boiled down to what certainly resembled a fundamentalism in many of these schools. Others, however, became tremendously sophisticated. There are some where the student can progress through school, into university, in what looks passably like a university campus, and emerge progressively with a BA, MA, or even PhD in Islamic studies. A great number of the Taliban high command came out of such schools. Their identifying marks were very often a war wound – one eye was common – and a madrassa diploma.

The question repeated here is related to that of a man who needs to travel with thousands of books – even while being hunted. How many books does it take to become a fundamentalist? Is it so simple – that which is taught and imbibed in year after year of study? If it were so simple, why is Osama so hard to understand, so difficult to predict? From 1998 the US has been trying to capture or kill him. Like the Scarlet Pimpernel of the first great Western revolution, he evades arrest and from time to time signals his health and activity by broadcasting something that is sufficiently coded for Western listeners to require a double-take, but which provides an image that goes straight to the heart of his Islamic listeners. The reference to Hubal is a case in point.

The US revenge for the Twin Towers

As if Osama knew that, after the Twin Towers, the US would come for him – and come to Afghanistan for him – and that the US would have to use the Northern Alliance armies that Ahmed Shah Massoud had rescued from Kabul, Osama had Massoud assassinated two days before 9/11. 'Cameramen', posing as a Belgian TV crew, had planted a bomb in their camera. Massoud took two days to die from his wounds. Whether he heard of the Twin Towers as he entered the last stage of dying is unknown. After his death, one of the key needs of the US in its push into Afghanistan was to unite the Northern Alliance. That it managed to do so was a considerable feat. Osama had rather been hoping that without Massoud the Alliance would fall into argument and faction.

As it was, even Osama probably did not know the precise date for the assault on the Twin Towers and Pentagon. The Al Qaeda cell system meant that its organizational matrix was like a spider's web. There was no normal organigram. A plan trickles into action via many untraceable detours. The web, even if it breaks in places, rebuilds itself. What Osama did know was that even if the US broke the web in Afghanistan it was now an international web. He might not know the precise dates of plans he had approved, but he knew that his organization could not be destroyed even if Afghanistan fell.

However, both Al Qaeda and the Taliban briefly fantasized that Afghanistan might not fall. And it is well to remember that notwithstanding Osama's influence over Omar the Taliban probably did not know that an attack on the US was planned. When it happened, and it was clear there would be a US response, the precedent of the Soviet failure cheered them. The only problem was that the Soviets were defeated mostly by attrition in the northern mountains, and those mountains were held by the Northern Alliance. A nervous Taliban awaited the US strikes. Against them their armies of AK47-wielding, sandal-wearing and Toyota-driving units, bulked up by a few almost derelict squadrons of Soviet tanks, would not stand long. For the US planners, however, Afghanistan was a God-send. Here was a terrorist headquarters contained in the borders of one state. Moreover it was a state whose strictures were so severe that it seemed universally unpopular. If there was a need for an instant reply after 9/11, Afghanistan provided the instant target. It allowed the second George Bush an avenue for action, and it allowed his planners to model the war along lines their computer programs could bear. The B52s were dusted off from Vietnam days, squadrons of high-tech aircraft were deployed, and the Northern Alliance would be the ground 'grunts' – accompanied of course by 'advisers', who would call in the airstrikes that would in turn allow the Northern Alliance to advance. Only in a few locations did the Taliban stand and fight, and that was usually when a strong Al Qaeda force was embedded with them. The foreign fighters had come precisely to fight. The Afghans, rather pragmatically, took to putting up token resistance and changing sides. The Students of God melted away, but the web of the spider, although punched through in Afghanistan, was not destroyed.

When the Twin Towers fell, the US was stunned by a great deal of the international response – which was decidedly unsympathetic to the US. In fact celebrations broke out in many parts of the world. It is well to remember that not all of this was a simple animosity towards the US. The French thinker, Bernard-Henri Levy, no longer able to shuttle between France and Ahmed Shah Massoud and act as the interlocutor of this part of the Third World, nevertheless dashed off a book that came out shortly after 9/11, entitled *Reflexions sur la Guerre, le Mal et la Fin de l'Histoire* ('Reflections on War, Evil and the End of History'). The preface is as ostentatious as ever, but perhaps prescient:

> [There are] other kamikazes ready to say to the nations of the world, 'You ignored us while we were alive; now we are dead; you didn't want to know about our deaths as long as they happened in our own countries; now we throw them at your feet, into the same fire that is consuming you. We who were invisible when alive will become clear to you as suicides.'[9]

The only problem here is not that the Third World as a pluralistic catchment of humanity is throwing up suicide bombers. It is one part of the Third World in particular - and that does not mean one country in particular - but something identifiably Islamic. That, in itself, is terribly unhelpful. What part of Islam, or what part within Islam, is identifiable? Scholars such as Fred Halliday have long argued that it is not Islam that confronts the West. Islam is too broad a term for a set of variant societies. But these variant societies face widely shared problems of development and the need for social and political change.[10] Is it then like the early Iranian revolution, with its mix of Islam and Third Worldism? Its mix of what part of Islam and what part of Third Worldism? Revenge for the Twin Towers did not begin to address these questions.

No simple or single reason

What follows is a hypothesis that cannot really be tested, and so is therefore suggestive. It may not be readily applied to Osama, if Ahmed Rashid is correct in reporting that he is impressionable, requiring mentors, and not intellectually consistent enough to sustain a complex view of how the world should develop.[11] If not, it may, however, apply to some of his mentors. It also takes some issue with Edward Said's observation that 'the gradual disappearance of the extraordinary tradition of Islamic *ijtihad* - the process of working out Islamic rules with reference to the Koran', in favour of rote learning, 'has been one of the cultural disasters of our time'.[12] It may not be that rote learning is all there is. It certainly takes issue with the clean and easy diagnostic distinction between 'secular' Islam and 'fundamentalist' Islam – as if it were simply one or the other – but a world view can contain a mixture of both the secular and the 'fundamental'. Certainly the association between Islam and Third Worldism is a case in point: here the secular and the complex cannot be weeded out. Books on 'Islamic' resistance to Western globalization are as much treatises on international political economy, and a Third World resistance in general, as an effort to privilege a special condition for Islamic countries.[13]

In brief, although Frantz Fanon must be seen as the original philosophical and psychological *animateur* of Third Worldism, most current Third Worldism gears off a theory of *dependencia*, or dependency, first articulated by Latin American theorists. The work of Raul Prebisch continues to have much influence,[14] although it must be said that the dependency 'school' is in fact a host of contending schools with a core critique. The detail of that core is itself contested, but essentially the theory posits a world divided between core and periphery – between metropolitan countries and the Third World – and capital accumulation at the periphery is dependent on the command of capital accumulation which emanates only at the core. Western globalization is only the latest developed manifestation of the core dictating to the rest of the world. Not only that, but accumulation at the core, insofar as it commands and controls capital accumulation at the periphery, requires the consent and cooperation of a *comprador* or collaborationist class of local elites and rulers. These are used and corrupted by the controlling classes at the global centres, which are in the West. The provision of oil and the control of the ownership of oil illustrate this part of the theory. It is thus a theory not only of international political economy, but a social critique of rulership. This double capacity of dependency theory allows its adherents simultaneously to criticize the West and the collaboration of Third World rulers.

Put at its crudest, dependency theory fits easily into a neo-
Marxist set of slogans to do with international class war. In fact it
can be packed easily into almost any set of slogans to do with
international dissatisfaction. However, there is a highly complex
side to the debate on dependency, and the line of thought Prebisch was originating 20 years ago is illustrative of this. Put most
simply, it says that only core capitalism can be *innovative*. Capitalism at the periphery can only be *imitative*. This takes the debate
beyond the question of 'who controls sovereignty?' into questions
as to how it is done. Prebisch outlined five key areas where the
Centre/the   Core/the   West   has   always   been   innova-
tive/first/original. These are to do with (1) technique and
consumption, whereby a sophisticated market not only consumes
more but participates in the techniques and technology of pro-
ducing more; (2) development and democratization, whereby
democratization has followed development, not the other way
around; only significant capital accumulation and capital stability
can facilitate democracy; (3) land tenure, whereby the reform of
land ownership in the West facilitated agricultural production
and surplus many years ago; (4) the formation of capital surplus,
whereby the Western Core has had sufficient surplus to distrib-
ute it in a manner that is approximately even, whereas
insufficient surplus in the Third World has resulted in corruption and, even without corruption, the formation of a dual
economy where some have but many have not; (5) population
growth, whereby the Western Core has stabilized its population
growth and hence its social structure.[15]

What this means is that, at best, the periphery is always
playing 'catch-up'. At worst it is playing catch-up in a game it
doesn't really want to play, particularly if the techniques of
production and consumption mean the fetishization and com-
modification of 'things' and their importance above spiritual
values. But, even if these five qualities have value in themselves,
the *political* question is raised as to why they cannot be achieved
through other means. Why must they be achieved only by *imitating* the West and by having rulers who seem slavishly devoted to
the West, and who are themselves rewarded but enslaved by this
devotion?

There are two other, sometimes contradictory, impulses at work here. They are present even within the Western debates on the international or global political economy. John Hobson has criticized Western political economists for trying to write the state out of their analyses, prioritizing global capital flows and transnational corporations. The state, he writes, is the only institution that can adapt to the various competing and shaping international forces, and shape them in turn.[16] Precisely because of this same judgement, what Islamic radicals seek is not only an *umma*, the transnational community of believers, but state reform (or revolution if need be), in order that Islamic states might play a stronger role in international relations and the international political economy. Osama wants the overthrow of the House of Saud, but he does not want the disappearance of Arabia.

The other impulse is to look beneath the level of the state. Susan Strange, in one of her final essays, wrote of the immense importance of civil society. By this she didn't just mean the polite non-governmental groupings normally associated with the term. She meant those who march and protest, those who discredit and despise politicians, those who hurl themselves against globalization at summits of world leaders.[17] This also is what Osama and the Islamic radicals want – only their 'civil society' is an Islamic one.

Of course there is one further and major, complex and largely secular, running sore in the radical agenda, and that is the question of Palestine. I say 'secular' because, despite the frequency of Islamic rhetoric, even Hamas knows that a solution, or at least a settlement, can only be negotiated on secular grounds: how much can be traded for how much. Its documents posit a complex Islamic justification for itself but, at base, Hamas is a nationalist organization. Article 12 of its Charter enshrines its commitment to nationalism, but notes that its nationalism is to be defended with Islamic devotion. 'A woman may go to war without her husband's permission and a slave without his master's permission.'[18] This goes beyond Islamic devotion as a mechanistic, at-command phenomenon. It suggests a devotion that is self-originatory. It suggests the autonomous *person* of Islam. What Palestine constitutes, however, is a *cause célèbre* to unite the Islamic world and all its persons, to identify a common enemy in the US as sponsor of Israel, and to criticize Arab leaders for having done so little for the Palestinians that, *as a last resort*, the Palestinians are blowing themselves up as suicide bombers. This has become of course the 'motif' of contemporary international *jihad* – the blowing up of one's self on another's territory, the 'notice us now, since you cannot now avoid noticing us' stratagem of Bernard-Henri Levy's indictment of the West. It has the dress of Islamic martyrdom. It is plotted like any NATO or CIA or MI6 or Mossad political/military stunt. Somewhere, someone has a 'ladder of escalation', where suicide in a marketplace is at a lower rung, and suicide against the Twin Towers is at a very much higher rung. But the choosing of oneself to be a suicide bomber nevertheless requires great self-will and determination.

What Palestine does is to bring the US, as ruler of the international political economy, that which must be imitated, into the foreground as oppressor of Palestine, that which can be very readily excoriated. The suicide bombs link both: locally, in the Israeli marketplace as a protest over oppression in Palestine; internationally, in the World Trade Center, symbolic home of the international political economy, as a protest against the way the world is run. If all this is merely 'fundamentalist' madness, well then, there is method in it, and complex method at that.

There is one final observation I want to make here, and it draws on the self-will suggested above. The complex methodologist who plans all this can only be a complex figure, or one of several complex figures. They may all espouse themselves as Servants of God, but they use God's gift of individual creativity and personality both to plan their operations and inspire those who carry them out. No one at least has doubted Osama's hugely charismatic capacity. The wish to have an *original* development, not merely an *imitative* one, broadcast into the world with such force, suggests an original and not imitative character behind it all. This is not Said's rote learning at work.

For hundreds of years Islamic theological and philosophical debate has been consumed with the nature of ontology – of selfhood and the free or other nature of selfhood. Drawing examples from medieval times, the eleventh century, we find that whether in the Arabic and Sunni tradition,[19] or in the Ismaili (tending Shia) literature,[20] the proposition has basically been that God is the 'Necessary Existent' and that any human claim to autonomy and subjectivity is impossible without recognition of the fact that each and every human is only a 'Contingent Existent', i.e. we have no prior claims to being autonomous and self-willed subjects; we generate autonomy and subjectivity only in terms of our relationship with what is truly prior, and that is God. Now this is very neat and can be used to justify or explain why it is that Islamic believers are driven by spiritual or religious authority, and how religious authority so easily influences political direction. In a 'fundamentalist' Islam, this neatness is absolute. The question to be asked, however, is whether Osama and other strongly willed activists and suicidists are so easily directed, or whether they themselves direct, over and above what a religious authority can command of them. Osama, after all, wound up determining Mullah Omar, not the other way around. In short, rather than being subjects of a fundamentalism, are they creatures of a certain autonomy, and do they carve for themselves an autonomous relationship with God? These are sacrilegious questions only in the context of a medievalism. The work of pioneering twentieth-century Islamic intellectuals may be instructive here.

Ali Shari'ati is regarded by many as the true ideological father of the 1979 Iranian revolution – before, that is, it was monopolized by the clerical faction.[21] A student in Paris in the 1960s, he was not only consumed by the notion that there could be a God-worshipping socialist, but was strongly influenced by the existential philosophy of Sartre. This was allied to the liberating emphases in Fanon's work, whereby it became the task of revolution to seek to create the 'whole man' whose birth Europe had either denied or had found impossible to facilitate. Shari'ati thought he could reconcile the idea of the free man, the whole man, i.e. the non-contingent man, with the idea of the free believer. Now in this Shari'ati was greatly helped by his Sufi version of Islam, where an individual can have a blinding union with God, i.e. an individual is free enough to enter union with

God, but a prisoner is not. In short, a certain mysticism permitted Shari'ati his ideas both of freedom and believerhood. Despite this, in the early days of the struggle against the Shah, it was Shari'ati's students who felt they had been best prepared for martyrdom. This did not come directly from Shari'ati's teachings but, by this time, his students had devised their own systems of thought and action, based on the foundations built by their teacher. This was martyrdom based on self-will and free-will. One freely chose, as a free individual, to die.

Osama is, of course, neither Sufi nor Iranian. He is not Paris-educated. But the influence of Fanon's writings as the genesis of Third Worldism has been widespread, and it is extremely difficult to disassociate Fanon from Sartre, at least from Sartre's long preface to *The Wretched of the Earth*, in which the act of revolutionary violence, even revolutionary murder, are pondered if not sanctioned. The idea of death is that one embraces it as a revolutionary act, not because it is Islamic. It is a revolutionary act that may then be given licence by a form of Islam, but the act is not in the first instance an act of a contingent being. It is, in Sartre's association with Fanon, an act of exemplary autonomy. And, if the death is an act of suicide, it is something which the West cannot imitate.

None of this may finally be Osama. It is an effort to hypothesize an Osama who is not simply evil and who is not simply 'fundamentalist'. He may well be 'fundamentalist' in many of his aspects, but he will certainly be complex in many others. If he runs a worldwide empire, he cannot be simple. If he runs it with sophisticated electronic communications, among other devices, he is not pre-modern. If he fought the Communists as well as the US, he is not a creature of any historical political bloc. He has commitment and tenacity. He has not been caught. If 'evil' is the only word that describes him, then it is evil of the medieval sort – able to conjure miracles of darkness without any other explanation being necessary. Freedom from explanation is not helping the cause of the West.

The response of the last men of history

History restarted very quickly. From the fall of the Berlin Wall in 1989 to the fall of the Twin Towers in 2001 was a very short dozen years. The First Man of restarted history seemed full of *thymos*, full of evil as well, and bereft of reason. The danger, in Fukuyama's rendition of Nietzsche, had been that the Last Men of accomplished history, that is of the triumph of Western history, would prove to be 'men without chests', soft and unable to defend themselves. Without gumption, they would let their history slip away. Perhaps they would have, like President Clinton after the bombing of US embassies in Africa in August 1998, fired 70 cruise missiles against targets in Afghanistan and killed 34 members of Al Qaeda, and done nothing more. To an extent, the first US demonization of Osama Bin Laden was also an effort on the part of President Clinton to divert attention away from the Monica Lewinsky affair, and also to name an all-purpose one-source cause of all international terrorism. In the past it had been Libya, for a brief time Iran. Now all international evil could be personified in Osama – the threat given a name, given an image, made flesh enough for one lucky bullet or cruise missile to put an end to him.

The response of the second George Bush to 9/11 was not simply to fire a few batteries of cruise missiles. He went on the offensive against both Osama and his hosts in Afghanistan. He took the Clinton tactic of sourcing evil, and the cause of 9/11, in the person of Osama and in his Al Qaeda organization, and he took the penchant and ability of his generals and defense secretary to wage war against a state enclosed by borders, possessing an army that could be defeated, possessing a government that could be overthrown, possessing in short the ingredients required for an eventual declaration of victory. It was fortuitous Osama had become so closely associated with Afghanistan. If he had melted into air, into an international and shadowy network of terror cells, against what could the US have struck? Against what tangible enemy and enemy space could it have declared victory? As it was, Afghanistan quickly fell, but Osama was neither captured nor killed, and Al Qaeda regrouped with speed. How does the US now strike at Osama? The answer is that it doesn't because it can't.

When the Twin Towers fell, a transatlantic storm briefly flared between intellectuals and academics. US scholars felt that their UK and European counterparts were too swiftly given to exercising a *schadenfreude* on behalf of their self-declared Third World colleagues – the entire 'you had it coming' syndrome. How would you feel, asked affronted US dons, if, instead of New York, suicide aeroplanes had plunged into the glittering spires of Oxford and Cambridge? And this was a very good question. There is an appalling ignorance in the UK, as well as the US, about the Third World in general and Islam in particular. If UK academics would not demonize Islam, they were prone to roman-ticizing it. Each requires a spectacular generality. At campuses across the UK, 'teach-ins' sprang up to explain how Islam was the 'Other' that the West required to complete its own self-image. Each image of virtue sanctifies itself by reference to a mirror image of evil. For the West, Islam was about to serve that func-tion of evil. Old copies of Edward Said's *Covering Islam* were dusted off to explain a contemporary history of Western media distortions of Islam.[22]

This was well and good. The problem was that there was so little said about an undistorted view of Islam. When it came down to it, despite (in the jargon derived from proto-disciplines such as post-colonial studies) the effort to 'gaze on difference', to 'gesture towards a solidarity', and to let 'the subaltern speak', almost no one spoke of Islam with nuanced knowledge. Everyone knew the Taliban had repressed women – so the Taliban mani-festly could not be defended. The Taliban had also blown up the giant fifth-century Buddhist statues in Bamiyan, but no one whispered that. For the Taliban too, there was not just one 'Other', the West, but many 'Others'. What could not be spoken of was passed over in silence. The rich history of the city of Herat was silenced in this discourse. The multiple Islams within Af-ghanistan alone were silenced. The semiotics of Mullah Omar sweeping the cloak of the Prophet about his own shoulders disappeared into the veil of ignorance.

In criticizing the US, and defending indiscriminately a gener-alized Islam, the left wing of academia created precisely its own version of Samuel Huntington's clash of civilizations. Academia may well have been rooting for the underdog in the face of US might – and indeed there is something not a little obscene about missiles and B52s making dust out of cities made of mud – but it did international understanding no good at all. Indeed, when the US moved on to Iraq, none of the platitudes of the 'Other' could serve in defence of the regime there. It was impossible to romanticize Saddam. By the same token, it was almost impossible to say that Saddam had anything to do with 9/11, with Osama Bin Laden, or with international terror. He was locally terrifying to be sure, but he had the misfortune to rule a state with geopolitical identifying marks such as borders. Indeed, he himself had tried to stretch those borders by invading first Iran, then Kuwait. Contained within those borders were weapons of mass destruction, of the sort that might be used to attack the West. 9/11 was now going to justify everything. Mind you, on 9/11 the terrorists had not used any Iraqi, Afghan or 'Other' weapons. It was US aeroplanes flown into US targets. Saddam also, unfortunately for him even if fortunately for the Iraqi people at some unplanned distant stage of the future, had those characteristics that could be demonized. A candidate for 'evilness', he was about to be upgraded from the 'B' list to the 'A' list of evil celebrity.

PART II

A SHORT HISTORY
OF THE AXIS OF EVIL

3 HISTORY'S LATEST SUPERPOWER GOES TO WAR AGAINST THE FIRST

In February 1991, after a massive Allied bombing campaign against Iraqi positions in Kuwait and southern Iraq, involving mostly US with some British and French warplanes, the first ground action took place. With symbolic staging in mind, it was Qatarian Arab troops who one evening crossed into Kuwait, staged a token engagement with some derelict Iraqi forces, then withdrew to a public relations victory. I was having dinner in Geneva with the Qatarian ambassador to Switzerland and, as with most modern wars, we ate while following the action on CNN. We talked about symbolisms. (I shall return, in the course of this essay, to symbolisms - one of which might include Qatar's hosting of Al Jazeera television as an uncomfortable portrayer of actual war and suffering in 2003.)

Of course, when the ground fighting broke out in earnest, symbolism took second place. It was there sufficiently for a nervous column of Kuwaiti soldiers to be almost bussed into Kuwait City, perched on board a fleet of armoured personnel carriers; but it was US forces who spearheaded the central drive into Iraq. To their west, British forces 'ran interference', guarding the US flank, and to the west of the British a flying wing of French forces advanced, ready to carry the thrust forward if the US and UK units were delayed by serious resistance. There was no serious resistance - although there was some serious slaughter of retreating Iraqi units by US gunships - but the entire advance was halted with probably nothing that could organizationally stand between the Allied advance and Baghdad. When British tanks encountered a Republican Guard tank squadron, the British cut through it like a knife through butter. On the second-last day of February, the first President Bush declared victory and an end to hostilities. Seventy-nine US soldiers had died (with a further 44 missing in action), 13 British, two French, and 13 Arab. The Iraqis lost between 200,000 and 700,000 soldiers, mostly from aerial bombardment. Kuwait had been liberated, but Saddam still ruled Iraq and proceeded to create mayhem among the northern Kurds and southern Shia. And, notwithstanding the participation of several Arab countries in the thrust against Saddam, including 15,000 Syrian troops, protests erupted in the streets of Islamic nations all over the world.

When, 12 years later, US troops finally entered Baghdad – with protests taking place all over the world and not only in Islamic nations – unaccompanied by any Arab allies, or any fighting allies at all apart from the British, the soldiers were stunned by the size and structure of Baghdad. For some it was the largest city they had ever been in. Many had no idea of its history. The Allied high command certainly had no idea it should seek to protect the antiquities contained in the museum, and these were looted – no doubt, eventually, to enter scattered private Western collections. Few knew they were in the country containing, at the confluence of the Euphrates and Tigris rivers, the Biblical site of the Garden of Eden – the garden that existed before evil was released into the world. Further south, the British troops seizing Basra probably had little sense that they were close to the original location for the story of Noah and his ark (although he was called Utnapishtim in the original Sumerian story). Outside Baghdad stood the partially restored ruins of Babylon, the site of mankind's first effort to organize itself independently of God (the Tower of Babel story) and later capital of the world's first superpower, with its great hanging gardens. The country gave rise to the first epic, of Gilgamesh's search for eternal life. And, again not too far from British operations, there had once stood a city named Ur, from which Abraham set out to establish himself as the founding father of both Jews and Arabs. Every contemporary human and political motivation, and a fair part of its political tribulations, not to mention the first writing and the first written laws (and some say the first rotational crop agriculture and the first water-sluiced domestic toilets[1]), came out of the land to which the flak-jacketed, sun-glassed and clench-jawed young soldiers had come.

An earlier young soldier

Of course this was not the direct descendant of all those pioneering glories. Tamburlaine, whose son established his capital in Afghanistan's Herat, swept through the area. Various Turkic peoples occupied or conquered what is now Iraq and, before the First World War and the advent of the British, the territory had been ruled – often quite loosely – by the Ottoman Empire for 400 years. It was against the Ottomans that Lawrence of Arabia had fought in the desert campaign. The young Oxford archaeologist with a passion for Crusader castles found himself leading a desert revolt and willingly set about thinking he could not only defeat the Ottoman Turks, but defy the British with their colonial plans. In the elegantly stilted, almost archaic, language of his famous memoir he confessed to trying to inflict fraud on both the Arabs (to induce them to support the British war effort) and the British (to induce them to recognize the Arab post-war claims). There cannot have been a more daring undertaking: with an army of mounted tribesmen, first help to defeat one great empire, then lead them to negotiate successfully with another, even greater. That he was even partially – by today's standards merely tangentially – successful is a testimony that outweighs all the Freudianisms and romances of his biographers. But he himself knew that he had failed. His epigrammatic poem says that he had wanted to build 'the inviolate house':

> But for fit monument I shattered it, unfinished; and now
> The little things creep out to patch themselves hovels
>   in the marred shadow
>   Of your gift.[2]

What Lawrence did was to help ensure that some Arab claims were at least partially met. Others were not. Those to do with what is now Iraq were not. It became one of the 'hovel' territories in 'marred shadow', and it took what is now called the 'Revolution of 1920' to persuade the British to abandon direct rule. They promptly took to stage-managing indirect rule, but the Iraqis were stubborn, and a lengthy dispute arose over oil in particular. Iraq was finally granted full independence in October 1932,[3] and one of the claims of the young nationalism was that the Iraqis were indeed directly descended from the splendid civilization of Babylon and Mesopotamia – years of intervention by a string of conquering peoples notwithstanding. The other ideological rubric was that of pan-Arabism. There was nothing, and would be nothing until the first Gulf War, about Islam as an identity. 'Iraq's main focus has been directed much more firmly at the Arab world than at the Islamic world.'[4] Indeed, all of Saddam's pre-war architectural projects had been Babylonian in conception – just as the Shah of Iran had sought to portray himself against the backdrop of Persepolis – and Saddam began a vainglorious restoration of the ruins of Babylon. His name was inscribed into an untold number of the new bricks, just so there was no mistaking who was responsible. It was quite clear why he was doing this: claiming a posterity for his country and personifying himself in it. The young Lawrence, whose affectations did not run far beyond Arab dress, would have been horrified.

The secular revolution and Saddam

It cannot be said that even after independence Iraq was free of British influence. Indeed, British reaction was a factor that loomed large in the calculations of every Iraqi government. These governments were not always stable, being an uneasy mixture of constitutional rule, monarchy and military power-broking. As in many other emerging Arab societies, young officers were actively propagating an ideology of pan-Arabism – the idea that centuries of division, and even the new century of state-formation, could be put behind them in favour of a new pan-Arab nation, stretching from North Africa to Iraq. This was a secular ambition, later taken up by people as disparate as Egypt's Nasser and Libya's Qaddafi. Simultaneously, in the newly independent Iraq, the idea of Babylonian heritage, i.e. of original civilization and culture long before Britain was even populated, grew strong. In a sense it gave pan-Arabism a long-term history. Yet it was also always a contradiction: Babylonian heritage helped a young Iraqi nationalism to grow strong, yet this nationalist strength had somehow to look towards its being merged into a pan-Arab nation, in the dreams of some visionaries a super-state. The binding cement was secularism, and the idea of autonomous progress built on autonomous history. A small Communist party began gaining adherents on the premise that faster material and secular progress was possible, and that a nation of socialist equality was within reach. When, during the Second World War, Britain and the Soviet Union formed a military alliance to fight Nazi Germany, the upshot in Iraq was greater freedom for the local Communist party to spread its influence. It was a combination of all these tendencies that confronted the post-war Iraqi monarchy and government.

These governments were not strong. Unprepared to govern a capital city, Baghdad, that had doubled in population from independence to the end of the war, and unable effectively to deal with the trade unionism that had arisen with industrialization and oil production, fractious within itself and given to repression, the government changed cabinets with lightning speed. Moreover, anti-government sentiment among the rapidly growing urban population was matched by anti-British fervour. Strikes were directed against British-controlled companies, and when, in 1948, war broke out in Palestine, the British were seen very much as blameworthy. The rise of Nasser in Egypt, together with his triumphant participation in the first great Third World summit in Bandung in 1955, and then particularly his staring down the British and the French over the Suez Canal in 1956, led many in the Arab world – including Iraq – to think an international paradigm change was in the offing. The British were on the wane, and so must be their corrupt client governments in the Arab Middle East.

Imitating what had happened in Egypt when Nasser assumed power, a secret group of younger military men calling themselves the 'Free Officers' overthrew the monarchy and government on 14 July 1958. One of the opposition parties that welcomed the coup was a group that was in effect the Iraqi branch of the Syrian Ba'th party. It stood for pan-Arabism and, to the Ba'th, now was the historical moment for union between Syria, Iraq and Egypt. The Arab nation would grow, and be an international force alongside the Third World in the wake of British decline. In later years Saddam never really abandoned this dream – with the exception that he wanted Iraq to be the leading Arab nation at the head of the Arab cause. Submerging Iraq into a wider union was not what he came to stand for. For him the Babylonian heritage was unique and pertinent to Iraq first and foremost. In 1958, however, the young Saddam was simply an ambitious official within a Ba'th that was just beginning to scent the possibility of power.

That rise to power was bloody. The first revolutionary governments were divided on the question of immediate union with Egypt and others in a United Arab Republic. The Communists in particular were cautious. The Iraqi opposition parties found it impossible to coalesce into a stable government and bitter faction fighting broke out. Some of this rapidly became intertwined with ethnic and tribal rivalries. Further overthrows or rebellions were plotted and suppressed. The suppressions were violent and bloody. Political massacres took place and the Ba'th, an early victim of these, plotted revenge – although it should be pointed out that the Ba'th had instigated unrest and assassination attempts on its own account.

The Iraqi leader who had emerged from the 1958 coup of the Free Officers and the immediate faction-fighting that followed was 'Abd al-Karim Qasim. He struck an entirely pragmatic alliance with the Communists, both being in no hurry to rush into a United Arab Republic. The Ba'th, with its Syrian origins and links, wanted union. It is not, however, as if this issue alone determined the unrest that followed. Iraq was a very weak state in terms of internal apparatus. All the nationalist talk of Babylon had not convinced the significant Kurdish population. And the art of government by Qasim, although it could alternate between the ruthless and the magnanimous, was also indecisive and opportunistic. On 7 October 1959 the Ba'th tried to assassinate him. The effort failed, although Qasim suffered extensive wounds. One of the assassins who escaped was the 23-year-old Saddam Hussein.

Thereafter the Ba'th plotted in secret. It formed alliances with nationalist officers with the intention of organizing another military coup. The Communists warned Qasim that a coup was in the air, but Qasim – who by this time had survived into the

beginning of 1963 – believed he had become genuinely popular.
In fact he had, but this did not protect him. On 4 February 1963
the military and Ba'th plotters moved. The people from the poor
quarters of Baghdad rallied to Qasim's defence, but they had no
weapons and Qasim was reluctant to give them any. For two days
the crowds fought the tanks with sticks and pistols. The coup,
though delayed in its success, nevertheless won through. Qasim
was given a summary trial and immediately executed. Between
February and November 1963 the Ba'th and its nationalist allies,
despite quarrelling bitterly, with each faction seeking ascendancy
over the other, exacted a terrible revenge upon its real and often
imagined opponents. The Communists in particular were ruth-
lessly suppressed.

Even so, it took until 1968 before a fully Ba'th government
won power. The years 1963 to 1968 were marked by extreme
intrigues, 'accidental' deaths and jockeying for position. The
country developed little in that time. When the Ba'th finally won
the power struggles, it was by ruthless jockeying. Two coups
occurred in July 1968. The first, on 17 July, brought a Ba'th-
influenced but almost gentlemanly government to power. The
second coup on 30 July was masterminded by Saddam Hussein.
Saddam was now effectively the Ba'th party leader, although he
took care not to occupy the very top positions. The party had
split from the Syrians in 1966 and, now, although content for a
time to be the power behind the throne – rather than visibly sit
on it – Saddam set out to lead the Iraqi Ba'th into a land and
ideology of its own.

> Despite his youthfulness, Hussein adjusted ably and quickly. He was
> realistic enough to know that holding on to his position, let alone
> moving forward to the presidential palace, would be a precarious
> and tortuous process. Yet he also was confident that he possessed
> the necessary qualities for this hazardous journey: great caution, end-
> less patience, intense calculation and utter ruthlessness.[5]

Saddam moved slowly but inexorably into a position of total
dominance of the Ba'th and, through it, of Iraq. In 1968 he was
assistant secretary-general of the party, then he became vice
president of the republic. Only in 1979 did he occupy the titular
eminence of president, party secretary-general, and commander-

in-chief. There was no doubt, however, throughout the decade preceding 1979, who was the supreme power in Iraq. Here it is important to balance the portrait of Saddam. He was ruthless, he deployed his power through the appointment of family members and fellow tribesmen from Tikrit, and he developed a formidable coercive apparatus and information network. An opponent of Saddam would fear for his life. Everything the US has said about his style of rule is either true or entirely credible. Simultaneously he and the Ba'th worked extremely hard finally to bring development to Iraq. Saddam was the architect of massive social welfare programmes; he greatly improved housing, education, and medical services; he established a modest form of social security, as well as a minimum wage and pension rights. It is fair to say that he did greatly reduce the gap between rich and poor. It is also accurate to say that it was he who removed the veil and immeasurably increased educational opportunities for women. Infrastructure developed, such as electricity and running water – and it worked. This meant much to Iraqi citizens, as US and UK troops in the Iraq of 2003 have discovered. Oil companies had been nationalized at a very early stage, and oil revenues financed all of this development, as well as the grandiosity of architecture that provided palaces for Saddam and declared an Arabic and Babylonian heritage in the public buildings of the country.

Thoughts of Arab union had by now disappeared from the Iraqi Ba'th. Arab leadership or at least regional leadership by Iraq became the precondition of any eventual and future union. Even so, much rhetoric took the place of actual policy. In 1970, during the ferocious Jordanian clampdown on the PLO – what came to be called 'Black September' – Iraq issued one statement after another of solidarity with the Palestinians but, despite 17,000 Iraqi troops with 100 tanks being already deployed in Jordan as part of an anti-Israeli front, Iraq fired not a single shot in defence of the PLO. The test of policy would come, not over Palestine, but over Iran. For when Saddam finally occupied all the formal titles of supreme office in Iraq, it was 1979. An Islamic revolution was taking place in neighbouring Iran and the US had grave concerns about an Iran that was left unchecked and unrestrained. In Iraq the secular government of Saddam Hussein no longer had any effective opposition and Saddam, despite blood unwashed from his hands, was at the height of what can be called a genuine popularity. Now was the time for both a regional test of leadership and an opportunity to forge an alliance with the US and other parts of the West. It should be pointed out that Iran is not an Arab country. What Saddam set out to accomplish, among other things, was a demonstration of Arab dominance over what was non-Arab. The fact that he was going to war with an Islamic country mattered not at all. When the going got tough, however, Saddam finally decided to play his own Islamic card.

War with Iran

The Iranian scholar Mahmoud Sariolghalam listed five elements that conditioned Saddam's foreign policy:

1. The virtual landlockedness of Iraq, with only modest access to the sea. This in itself might have provoked tensions, if not conflicts, with neighbours having greater sea access.
2. Iraq's strategic desire to command a greater space within the Persian Gulf.
3. Iraq's self-declared ambition to command a leadership role in Arab politics.
4. The Kurdish problem in northern Iraq required a caution with Iraq's northern neighbours.
5. Iraq's heterogeneous ethnic, political and confessional groupings meant that any of these groups might find allies in neighbouring countries, e.g. the Iraqi Shia might find commonalities with the Iranian Shia.[6]

Here elements 1, 2 and 5 all involved Iran. Elements 1 and 2 were almost predestined by the long-running dispute between Iraq and Iran over the ownership of various islands and navigation rights in the Shatt al-'Arab waterway. The withdrawal of Britain had left a naval vacuum in this part of the Gulf, and in November 1971 Iran occupied the two Tunbs islands and the third island of Abu Musa. The Ba'th, at this stage having barely consolidated its position and with internal rivalries occupying much of its time, had no reply to make to the Iranian action,

apart from deporting some 50,000 'Iranians', including many
who had been settled in Iraq for generations. The Ba'th had
continuing internal problems with the Kurds, in terms of element 4 and in terms of a united Iraq, and it had especial
problems with element 3.

Isolated from the Syrian Ba'th, who now viewed its Iraqi
namesake as politically heretical, and almost completely uncon-
sulted by other Arab powers over the October 1973 war with
Israel, Iraq's response was petulant. It refused to join in the oil-
price-rise war that followed. That rise in oil prices effectively
elevated Saudi Arabia into a major Arab player, which promptly
set about recycling many of its petrodollars in the United States.
When, in November 1977, Egypt's President Sadat made his
historic visit to Jerusalem, it seemed that US policy was embedded in the region. When Saddam finally decided to assume the
Iraqi presidency in 1979 he had some clear strategies before him.

Firstly, he had to recover Tunbs and Abu Musa from the
Iranians. Secondly, he had to take the fight to the new Iranian
regime, and perhaps secure the support and approval of the US
who were alarmed by the 'fundamentalism' of the Ayatollah and
the clerics. Thirdly, in doing so, he could once again widen the
pan-Arab credentials of his regime. He made much of a great
battle in 637, when Arab Muslims decisively defeated the then-
non-Muslim Sassanid Persians at Qadisiyya, and he did score at
least a 'limited legitimizing point when he boasted that the battle
with Iran, joined in September 1980, would soon yield another
"Qadisiyya".'[7] That battle with Iran turned into an eight-year war
of appalling attrition, damage and loss of life.[8] Although Western
arms and money did find their way to Saddam – often very large
amounts – the West was in general concerned not to be too
publicly associated with him, notwithstanding the fact that the
West was also delighted that the new Iranian regime was being so
preoccupied.

Iran, however, probably won the propaganda battle, at least
for a time. Trading on the fact that Iran's was a revolutionary
Islamic regime, and Iraq's was pointedly secular – and had been
for all its modern history – the Ayatollahs depicted Saddam as a
kufr, an unbeliever, no better than Ronald Reagan, and this

demonization fell on many receptive ears in the Muslim world. Saddam had to regroup his justifications: he once again began making much of his support for the Palestinians, and he elevated his ranking in the Arab world by the tactic of denigrating others, particularly those *nouveau riche* states that had grown prosperous on the back of selling oil at high prices to the West, such as Kuwait and Saudi Arabia (whereas Iraq had not joined the oil-price war), and which, in the case of Saudi Arabia, now hosted US bases and military personnel in great numbers. Saddam never used the term 'Hubal', as Osama Bin Laden later brilliantly did. But, in this way, Saddam tried to win US support while elevating Iraq above other US allies. For what Saddam wanted was not to be an ally, but to have his Arab-leadership ambitions understood if not at least tacitly underwritten by the US. Now he set about to combat the Ayatollahs' propaganda about him and to establish some Islamic identity for himself – as the spokesman/defender of Arab lands against foreign occupation: against the US military 'occupation' of Saudi Arabia, with all its holy places; against the Israeli occupation of Palestine with its own holy sites in Jerusalem; against the financial and economic colonization of entirely collaborationist regimes such as that in Kuwait.

By the end of the war with Iran it was probably honours even in the propaganda war, but, for the first time, Saddam had resorted to Islamist self-portrayal as well as one based on Arab history. And thinking, as he had in his climb to the top in Iraq, that he could, even if contradictorily but successfully, play off different parties to his advantage, he considered that the US must regard itself, despite Iraqi criticisms of the US, as in some way beholden to Iraq for its tying down for almost a decade the fundamentalist regime in Iran.

But it was not as if Saddam abandoned his efforts to formulate a national history that was entirely unique. The triumphal arch of crossing scimitars was erected to celebrate 'victory' in the war against Iran. Memorial services for the Iraqi fallen were held in Babylon, and Saddam announced an architectural competition for the restoration of the hanging gardens of Babylon, opening up this competition to Western architects.[9]

None of this grandiosity, however, could hide the economic impact on Iraq of the war against Iran. Although Saddam had balanced his international and domestic expenditures rather well, his finances were sufficiently parlous – but not precarious – for him to find it difficult to continue his quest for Arab pre-eminence and domestic development. It was at this point that he began, quite conspicuously, to pick a quarrel with Kuwait. He demanded an immediate decrease in 'excessive' Kuwaiti oil production in order to protect Iraq's own share of the market. Tensions with Israel grew, and Arab states seemed reluctant to make available large grants for Iraqi post-war reconstruction. Mahmoud Sariolghalam is of the opinion that, in the mix of objective and subjective judgements that formed Saddam's decision making, the subjective won out, 'preoccupied' as he was 'with his interpretations, inferences and outlook'.[10]

Perhaps this is how he misread what he thought were US signals that an Iraqi invasion of Kuwait would meet no serious obstacle. The signals from Washington that Saddam was reading seemed to him to say that 'the US government has no opinion on inter-Arab rivalries'.[11] Those rivalries, as the US would have known had it traced them in detail, included episodes of bitter history between Iraq and Kuwait. The first revolutionary leader of Iraq, Qasim (whom Saddam as a young man had tried to assassinate), had tried and failed to annex Kuwait in 1961. For many years Iraq had seen Kuwait and the other small Gulf sheikhdoms as an anomaly in the region, caused by colonialism and the desire of the decolonizing powers to guarantee their oil supplies by spreading the number of suppliers and locating the supplies in tiny and perhaps dependent territories. They did not prove dependent, especially after the 1973 oil price rises, but they did remain loyal to the West. In more than one way, the use of Qatarian troops to lead the first land battle with Iraq in the first Gulf War was apposite. Not only was Qatar an Arab state with an Islamic population, but it was itself one of the tiny sheikhdoms viewed as anomalous by Saddam. In the prelude to the Gulf War, however, Saddam thought he would cut through the Gordian Knot of his problems at a stroke: annexing Kuwait would resolve his economic problems, overcome the colonial legacy, send an undisputed signal to the Arab world that it should view Iraq more favourably, and give Iraq an unrivalled oil-production base with which it could then talk on equal terms with the West. And, on top of all this, the US seemed not minded to interfere. On 2 August 1990 Saddam marched into Kuwait. It was certainly bold, but equally misjudged.

The first Gulf War

Not a single Arab state supported the invasion of Kuwait. This is what allowed the US eventually to form its coalition against Iraq. There was a uniform feeling that unilateral invasions and annexations could not be tolerated. This is why even Syria played a role in the coalition. Not only that but Saddam, in seeking to up the *ante* dramatically and swiftly, probably miscalculated again. On 3 August 1990 14 of the 21 Arab League foreign ministers met in Cairo and condemned the Iraqi invasion. Only Libya objected to the condemnation. On the same day, however, Saddam massed his troops on the border with Saudi Arabia. If the US had no immediate pretext for intervention in the rapidly moving but brief scenario to date, Saddam now provided it. On 7 August the US responded to a Saudi request for help by sending troops and aircraft. Operation Desert Shield was effectively under way five days after the invasion, backed at this stage by two UN Security Council Resolutions (660 and 661) threatening military force and imposing economic sanctions.

On 8 August Saddam simultaneously announced the formal union of Iraq and Kuwait and said that he would not attack Saudi Arabia. This assurance, however, was too late. On the same day, Britain announced it would send warplanes to the Gulf, France strengthened its naval presence there and, on 10 August, 12 of the 21 Arab League members voted to send troops to defend Saudi Arabia. A day later Syria announced it would do the same, but already on that day Egyptian and Moroccan troops began landing in Saudi Arabia. It must be said that this all took place at lightning speed by the standards of both UN and Arab diplomacy. A week and a half had not yet elapsed since the invasion. The coalition against Saddam seemed to form without any need for arm-twisting and pressure. Libya aside, the Arab states found the issue crystal clear. You cannot unilaterally invade

and annex a sovereign state with recognized international personality under international law, and one Arab state should
certainly not do this to another Arab state.

Saddam saw that he had overstepped the mark. He immediately sought to buy time, to widen the issues at stake and, having
lost the political support of Arab governments, made a play for
popular opinion in both Arab and other Islamic countries. On
12 August Saddam said he would withdraw from Kuwait on
condition that the Israelis withdraw from Gaza, the West Bank
and the Golan Heights; that the Syrians withdraw from Lebanon;
that, albeit under UN auspices, Arab troops should replace
'foreign' troops in Saudi Arabia; that UN Security Council
resolutions condemning Iraq should be withdrawn, but that
resolutions applying to Israel and Palestine should be imple-
mented. In no way, with such a wide variety of disparate actors
and issues involved, was this a serious or even possible negotiating position. The aims, if there were any, were to detract popular
support from the Arab governments now ranged against him,
declare he was making a stand against Israel for the benefit of the
Arab and Islamic world, play for time and hope that the US and
its coalition allies would not attack. The various ruses of diplomatic expulsions, human shields, invitations to distinguished
figures to mediate in both the hostage issue and in the larger
stand-off, were to mix pressure and the appearance of concilia-
tion, to divide Western public opinion by appealing to anti-war
sentiments, and to buy time. It certainly caused a huge number
of genuinely popular demonstrations to spring into life in many
Islamic countries, and these all criticized the US and defended
Saddam. To be fair to Saddam, he played good defensive chess,
but his opening gambits had already ruined his position. The
war, when it came, came with the inevitability that was inescapa-
bly built into Saddam's misguided invasion of Kuwait.[12]

The subsequent history of the war is well known. What I have
sought to do here is to state that a political and legal case was
properly established for coalition action in the first Gulf War. It
was a political and legal case that drew immediate agreement and
support from Arab and Western governments alike. UN resolutions were broadly supportive of the military action that followed,

and, to his credit, the first President Bush did not seek to drive his troops to take Baghdad; he did not in this way exceed what the resolutions had provided for. Saddam certainly learned that a Korean-War-vintage army could not stand up against the mobility and technology now possessed by Western forces, and he could not have regrouped in time even to try. In brief, despite the coalition victory, despite the 'triumph of history', Saddam survived. The political and legal case had, in any case, reached its limit. The Arab partners in the coalition would have been placed in an impossible position if their Western colleagues had taken Baghdad, and the UN resolutions were specifically against the Iraqi invasion of Kuwait – they did not call for Iraq's overthrow.

What, however, about the ethical case for going to war? I ask this question because, when it came to the second Gulf War 13 years later, there was not a clear-cut political and legal case. There was certainly no fighting coalition that sprang into place based on political and legal conviction, and certainly none with any Arab participation. The second war was premised on an ethical argument: better to contain the evil now than seek to face it after it has gained strength in the future. I shall examine that ethical argument later. Was there, however, an ethical argument for the first war?

The concept of a 'just' war has been embedded in a highly particular way in Western thought since the time of St Augustine, writing round about the year 400. Basic principles such as legitimate authority to declare war, just cause, proportionality – so that the damage done by war is not greater than the damage that caused war in the first place – and war as a last resort all came from Augustine, with a later gloss by St Thomas Aquinas.[13] More recent thought on just war has come from Michael Walzer, who adds a complex form of utilitarianism to the debate on what is just or not, and I shall discuss some of his contribution below. Walzer aside, however, the Augustinian origin of thought on just war suggests a highly Christian animation of the debate. There is certainly an Islamic vision of just war, and that underlies all concepts of a *jihad*, no matter how loosely or carelessly various clerics use the term.[14]

The Augustinian principles are used here, however, for two reasons: insofar as they are used in Western discourse to justify why the West went to war, and insofar as these principles have essentially embedded themselves in the Geneva conventions that give the modern world its universal laws of war. In this context the debate over whether the first Gulf War, as fought by the West and its allies, was just or not hinges on one particular principle. There was legitimate authority in the form of UN resolutions and a clear universal condemnation from the world's states of the Iraqi action. There was just cause, and that was to overcome Iraq's unjust and illegal action. The issue of proportionality is more cloudy – the Iraqi army took a far greater pounding than was required to break its fighting resolve – but George Bush's restraint in pulling his forces back from the road to Baghdad fulfilled a key requirement of proportionality: it reversed the offence; there was an invasion, and the invasion was repulsed; there was no additionality, no going further than repulsion of the invasion, no march on Baghdad. The debate tends to come down, basically, to the principle of last resort. Was war really the last resort, or could more have been done to achieve the aim of Iraqi withdrawal without war? This of course was an active message being sent by Saddam – that negotiation was possible – but this does not by itself invalidate the question.

A.J. Coates points out the different emphases even within the West. Most European states expended immense diplomatic energies seeking a negotiated compromise with Saddam, whereas the US and UK were adamant in demanding an unconditional withdrawal. Part of the former approach certainly anchored itself on sanctions, which were to be combined with ongoing diplomacy. But this 'appears to exaggerate the efficacy of sanctions and of diplomacy and to underestimate the costs of further delay. However, at the end of the day, much depends on political and military judgements, which by their nature are uncertain, inexact and, therefore, highly contestable.'[15] Coates actually sets up two tests here: the first is to do with the proportionality of cost (would delay cause more pain and cost than swift action?); the second is to do with political judgement, contestable and inexact as it is, being a foundation for moral judgement (if political

judgement says 'act now', is immediate action then also moral?).
Neither test is going to provide an unambiguously clear answer,
so that even someone like Richard Norman, a philosopher
obviously unhappy about the first Gulf War, is forced to prevari-
cate. A negotiated solution would have been, he says, 'morally
much more acceptable', would have saved countless lives and
provided a methodology for future crises. However, 'if sanctions
or negotiations are only partially successful, and if a refusal to
resort to war leaves no alternative but to make significant conces-
sions to the aggressor, this may encourage future acts of
aggression.'[16] Norman finally concedes that this intractable bind
– since one cannot tell the future when one embarks upon an
action – can only, in the case of Iraq and Kuwait, be addressed by
the historical knowledge that invasion almost always creates a
more oppressive government than that which existed before.
That at least provides a ground for military inaction – not that a
sovereign state is sacrosanct in itself, but that the condition of a
sovereign state should not be made worse.

This is ingenious and only partially helpful. After all, Tanza-
nia invaded Idi Amin's Uganda to the betterment of Uganda and
the Ugandans. Vietnam invaded Cambodia and put an end to
the terror of the Khymer Rouge. The first George Bush tried to
ameliorate the situation in Somalia by invading that country, and
it was the attrition caused by anarchy and resistance that defeated his intention, rather than the intention being necessarily
wrong in itself. But the Norman formula does point a way out of
the impossibility of predicting what proportion of good or evil
will attend either one of alternative but difficult actions. It says
that arguments over whether it really is 'the last resort' can never
be satisfactorily answered.

Michael Walzer provides more practical help with a series of
clear distinctions in the preface to the second edition of his
famous work.[17] Walzer acknowledges the difficulties of determining just proportion ahead of time. He makes the fundamental
point that a just war has to be a limited war, i.e. it is tied to a just
aim, a definable just cause. Once that aim or cause is satisfied the
remit of justice has come to an end. Thus it is possible to support
a war to throw Iraq out of Kuwait, *without* simultaneously being

in support of a 'new world order' or the 'end of history' that are
rhetorically added to the original rationale. It is also possible to
support a war which is justly fought, rather than a war that turns
to butchery, i.e. to support the war against Iraq is not also to
support the slaughter of large numbers of fleeing Iraqi troops in
what was called a 'turkey shoot'. Walzer, it should be added,
turns his argument on fine distinctions which, frankly, can
sometimes go either way. For example, if fleeing Iraqi troops live
to fight and kill another day, what good has been accomplished
by sparing them? Probably the most contentious, but most interesting, of Walzer's points is that 'justice is not the whole of
morality'.[18] Walzer expresses uneasiness that it was 'just' – as I
have discussed above in terms of just-war criteria – to throw Iraq
out of Kuwait and not to go on to Baghdad and overthrow
Saddam. However, was letting Saddam continue as a tyrant in
any way moral?

In a sense this gets to the heart of original Augustinian
thought. This was not, after all, merely a construction of lists of
principles. It is not Walzer but Paul Ramsey who cites a key part
of Augustine's *City of God* (Part XIX): 'For it is the wrongdoing of
the opposing party which compels the wise man to wage just
wars', often against his will and inclination, 'and this wrongdoing, even though it give no rise to war, would still be a matter of
grief to man because it is man's wrongdoing.' Augustine adds
that anyone who thinks there is not a hard moral conundrum
here – to go to war justly though grievously, or not go to war yet
be grieved that wrongdoing is being perpetuated – who seeks to
bury his head in the sand, 'thinks himself happy because he has
lost human feeling'.[19] There is a choice to be made here, guided
by principles of justice perhaps, informed by proportionality, if
these can be assessed, but finally reduced to a simple question of
whether humanity can be happy if it allows wrongdoing – if it
allows evil – to flourish in the world. And this is the key to the
arguments put forward in the US and UK to justify the second
Gulf War. Many of the arguments were tendentious – not so
much to do with just war as justified war – and nothing was fully
convincing, either to do with Saddam's threat to the West or
ddam's threat to his region or even Saddam's threat to his own

country (why more threatening now than over the last several years?). No Arab state bought into the justifications, and France and Germany pointedly resisted them. Except briefly when fighting started, popular opinion even in Britain never fully accepted the government's case, and a huge furore broke out as to the extent the government had in fact exaggerated its case for war. The key to the US and British insistence on war, despite ambiguous or non-existent support from international law, and huge international scepticism, was that Saddam was evil, and that it was not moral to allow this sort of evil to exist in the world.

The evil of mass destruction?

When the French foreign minister, Dominique de Villepin, made his stirring speech in the UN Security Council against the 2003 war with Iraq, he was also finishing writing his new book on poetry and poets, and a specific sort of poet – people like Rimbaud, people who in their time were regarded by polite society as outsiders, as mad, as possessed by genius perhaps but also by evil.[20] This may seem an absurd subject for a pillar of the French establishment, representing France at what was meant to be the pillar of international diplomacy. What de Villepin was saying at the Security Council, however, was that there would be something absurd in promising a new Iraq simply on the basis of destroying the old. Who knew what historians and critics may one day say? Invasion had to be just; it had, in time-honoured argument, to be a last resort, and it had to lead to something new and better. The last condition was something no Western power had yet planned properly, prepared for or rehearsed.

There were words of course about a better society afterwards. Some were echoes. In 1917 the commander of the British forces in Iraq, General F.S. Maude, had said: 'Our armies do not come into your cities as conquerors or enemies but as liberators. Your wealth has been stripped of you by unjust men, the people of Baghdad shall flourish under institutions which are in consonance with their sacred laws.'[21] I have outlined above the subsequent history of Iraq, where unjust man succeeded unjust man. In 1991 the first President Bush argued that going to war with Saddam would make the world a safer place. The tragedy of the Twin Towers, ten years later, has not been evidence of that.

Locating evil, locating the lack of international safety in the identities of single men or single organizations or single states has not quarantined evil.

What the emphasis on single men such as Osama and Saddam has done is to have focused attention on what they stand for: not fundamental Islam or a reprise of Babylon, but something more than that. I argued earlier in this essay that in the mixture of religious and secular thought that animates what is loosely called Islamic fundamentalism, there is both an adherence to the idea of an Islamic international civil society (a radical version of which Osama stands for) and simultaneously a desire to see the emergence of strong Islamic states able to play a meaningful role in international relations (and this is the image Saddam consistently sought to play on behalf of Iraq). Destroy Osama or destroy Saddam and you may well destroy something called 'evil', but you will also destroy peculiar but real symbols of an emergence into international relations that is not powerless. Using your power to destroy this will only encourage those re-identified as powerless once again to loose their powerlessness. Islam must be allowed a symbol in the world, and I shall return to that.

Returning to the echo of General Maude's speech, in the wake of the latest 'beneficial' invasion of Iraq what, more than a year after the March 2003 invasion, is the situation for Iraqis? Utilities such as electricity and water took agonizingly long months to restore and are still not fully reliable. They have no effective domestic security and banditry is rife. In a country where weapons are plentiful, Baghdad alone runs to some 400 homicides per week. In a country where medical facilities are under-provisioned and overstretched, the hospitals cannot cope and the mortuaries are full of bodies. US soldiers are not preventing the sabotage and bombings caused by a regrouping of Saddam's forces, but are conspicuously bullying and shooting Iraqi citizens and foreign journalists – the Abu Ghraib prison abuses are a case in point. The country's prize antiquities previously housed in Baghdad's museums have been looted. Hospitals and schools have also been looted. There has been no explosion of literary and cultural joy and experimentation of the sort that briefly happened after the Iranian revolution. A surly, war-weary population endured what it considered occupation, happy perhaps that Saddam had gone, even happier after his capture at the end of 2003, but now nationalistic and Iraqi enough to think of their nationalism as having been defaced. After all, the powers that have now come are the same powers that insisted on the maintenance of Iraqi sanctions that stretched from the first to the second Gulf Wars. However Saddam used these sanctions to his own benefit – and he did – those on the receiving end were those who found themselves looking upon the tanks and sunglassed young men from the sending end.

Returning to Dominique de Villepin's UN speech, what was the background of caution against war that animated de Villepin and France, and which more than a year on still acts as a chastening note to the US and British action?

1. There has been no evidence of weapons of mass destruction able to attack the West, let alone attack the West in a sustained and coordinated manner.
2. There has been no evidence of weapons of mass destruction able to dominate the region. After all, if Iraq had gone to war again with Iran at the very beginning of 2003, it would have had no military edge to speak of.
3. There has been no evidence of weapons of mass destruction able to target Israel, let alone attack Israel in such a way that Iraq could avoid massive Israeli retaliation.
4. There may have been programmes to develop weapons of mass destruction, but there is no evidence of military doctrine for their use. Would they have been automatically used for aggression or for deterrence?
5. There was no evidence that Saddam's rule of Iraq was any worse than in the preceding 13 years. If anything, sanctions had made Saddam stronger and more unchallengeable than ever. Ordinary Iraqis were worse off, but Saddam was widely seen as the man who had guided the nation through sustained economic pressure from the West.
6. There was no evidence of any move on Saddam's part to attack the autonomous Kurdish enclaves in Iraq's north.

7. There was no evidence of any move on Saddam's part to attack either Iran or Saudi Arabia.
8. There was no evidence of extraordinary support on Saddam's part for Hamas or other radical Palestinian groups, certainly nothing on a par with Syrian support.
9. There was no evidence of any links, and certainly no continuing operational links, with Al Qaeda or Osama Bin Laden.
10. There was no evidence that Saddam had been even remotely involved in preparations for 9/11.

In its own preparations for war, at the same time as the French were resisting the move to war, Britain searched for details that would substantiate the case for war, and war in the first part of 2003. One week before the British prime minister released what was meant to be a defining dossier of reasons for war, his own chief of staff, Jonathan Powell, was writing a memorandum dated 17 September 2002 to the chairman of the British Joint Intelligence Committee:

> First the [draft dossier] document does nothing to demonstrate a threat, let alone an imminent threat from Saddam. In other words it shows he has the means but it does not demonstrate he has the motive to attack his neighbours let alone the west. We will need to make it clear in launching the document that we do not claim that we have evidence that he is an imminent threat.[22]

No such reliable evidence, despite claims to the contrary, was ever gathered. The war, when it came – starting with a daring effort at the aerial assassination of Saddam on the evening of 19/20 March 2003 and 'ending' with the symbolic toppling of Saddam's statue on 9 April – had no clear UN endorsement (although the US and Britain used a contentious and narrow interpretation of UN resolutions) and therefore no unambiguous legitimate authority. It had no overwhelming just cause, despite inflated dossiers, i.e. it answered no specific and immediate offence. It had no proportionality in the sense that Saddam had not threatened the overthrow of any other government, but he was himself overthrown. There probably is, in this case, a strong argument to be made that the 'last resort' had not yet been reached, given the ongoing work of Hans Blix and his UN weapons inspectors. In no standard Augustinian sense was the war just. Whether, in Michael Walzer's caveat or Paul Ramsey's wider sense of Augustine, the war was unjust but moral is the question that must now be posed.

There are two immediate observations I should like to make. The first is to do with the British prime minister's sense of argument. This seems to answer the question 'why now?', i.e. why go to war against Saddam in 2003 when he has been a tyrant for many long years? The sense of argument seemed to be that, yes, Saddam has done nothing more conspicuously evil in recent times than in past times but, because he is evil now in the same sense as he was then, the case against Saddam is that he is *intrinsically* evil, and what seemed to become the prime minister's personal crusade - against all European and Arab advice - was a crusade against intrinsic evil.

The second observation concerns the US defense secretary, Donald Rumsfeld. For Rumsfeld, Saddam represented an evil, as it were, within frontiers, i.e. Iraq could be identified in geopolitical and geostrategic terms. Within those terms and frontiers, Rumsfeld - against the advice of his generals - thought he could 'shock and awe' the Iraqis into surrender through a huge display of unanswerable technology, a massive attack against which the Iraqis could make no reply. As it turned out, the generals were vindicated when the Iraqis did indeed attempt a reply by harassing the long lines of logistical support the US troops required as they slogged up the desert roads to Baghdad. This part of the war, with its strategies of supply and harassment, was little different to wars in ancient Babylon. But in Rumsfeld's original vision, technology could vanquish evil. Neither Rumsfeld nor any other part of the US administration made detailed plans for the aftermath of war. There were vague political ideas about interim US rule, with a US-selected cadre of Iraqi exiles and opposition leaders,[23] but no logistical plans about providing public utilities, public medical support, public security, cultural security, or any of the wherewithals of actually making a country work. Against advice and pleas from aid organizations not to bomb electricity and water stations, the high-tech US bombing did precisely that. The absence of administrative plans was staggering, and the poor start the US made to running the country is very precisely the US's fault. It is as if it was a foregone conclusion that with the defeat of evil, evil would automatically be replaced by good. This was in part due to the ascendancy of the Rumsfeld hawks over the more moderate Colin Powell, but it was all the same Manicheanism in its crudest form. It had its own recent intellectual history. There was the residue of Fukuyama's use of Hegel. Under Hegel's Spirit of Fulfilled History, the Spirit of Good would automatically fill the vacuum left by the ousting of the Spirit of Evil.

Doctrines

Saddam had learnt from the first Gulf War that his forces could not stand up against the technologized power of the West. In that war he had positioned his armies to defend Iraqi borders, and they were simply bombed into surrender. Subsequent isolated encounters between Western forces and Republican Guard tank squadrons ended badly for the Iraqis. In the second Gulf War it appeared that Saddam was going to deploy a guerrilla campaign. The hit-and-run harassment of Western units and supply lines – allowed to cross the borders with relative ease – suggested that Saddam would continue this strategy within Baghdad itself. This time it seemed it would be a defence in depth, and in irregular depth, rather than in massed regular formation on the borders. Then Saddam appeared to make a major mistake. Although leaving it as late as possible, he ordered or sanctioned the massing and deployment of his elite Republican Guard and Special Republican Guard regiments on the outskirts of Baghdad. The Western high command was delighted – and relieved – and once again promptly bombed them into an ineffectual rump of what they could have been had they fought the Western invaders street by street. Technology would not have been a great advantage in such circumstances. Perhaps Saddam was stupid. Perhaps he could not bear to see his beloved Baghdad destroyed in street-by-street fighting. As it was, the greatest damage to Baghdad came from Western bombing and air strikes – the effort to 'shock and awe'.

The notion of 'shock and awe', although the term had been a speechwriter's coinage (as had 'Axis of Evil' and 'War on Terror'

before it), was seriously subscribed to by Donald Rumsfeld and
his new generation of hawks in Washington. In Rumsfeld's mind
it was more than a notion, and was itself a doctrine: that unanswerable technology, coupled with unanswerable speed (the latter
facilitated by technology), would leave any enemy devastated,
breathless and unable to keep up. Massive regular deployment
was obsolete and, as a result of not needing such deployments,
the US could intervene militarily with speed in any location or
many locations. Not only that (here the speechwriters become
almost as important as the weapons), but the swift technology of
destruction and intervention would allow the US a 'full-spectrum
dominance' of the post-Cold War world. It was a doctrine more
than a decade late in coming, years after the fall of the Berlin
Wall, but this was the doctrine both to guarantee that history
had indeed ended on Western terms and that the Huntingto-
nian line in the sand that demarcated Western civilization could
be drawn so far forward that enemies would effectively have no
geopolitical and geostrategic space of their own.

Under 'full-spectrum dominance', evil would be rooted out of
all the dominated world, and a Pax Americana would rule that
world. It was all curiously reminiscent of John Foster Dulles and
his 'massive retaliation' - only non-nuclear 'shock and awe' were
now the substitute words. It was also something that imbibed the
post-Dulles quest for a ladder of escalation that was not too
swiftly nuclear. The advances in military technology meant that
finally there was a range of devastating alternatives to nuclear
weaponry both in the early stages of grand conflict but, since
there was no longer a grand enemy such as the Soviet Union,
especially in all foreseeable stages of smaller-scale conflict.

Unlike the post-Dulles Kennedy/Healey/Schmidt era, the
doctrine was no longer merely to contain an enemy, to give up
on the idea of victory, to have a safe world based on mutual
deterrence and, to that extent, mutual respect, but to dominate
the world and to impose Western if not US values upon it.
Unlike Huntington's proposed limits - a line drawn to exclude
or isolate the Islamic world - Rumsfeld proposed to dominate
the Islamic world as well. However, since the doctrine demanded
the diminution of geopolitical space to those opposed to West-

ern or US values, the campaign for domination had to take place geopolitical space by geopolitical space. This is why it made sense to 'make an example' of Iraq – both unfinished business from the first Bush era, and the start of a new business entirely. It didn't really matter if the UN did not provide 'legitimate authority' for war. Legitimate authority was also part of what was possessed under full-spectrum dominance.

If this was a chilling assertion of self on behalf of the world's only superpower – that it was now setting about becoming an omnipower – what was almost assiduously sad was the buy-in on the part of the British prime minister. It cannot be said that this was necessarily against the grain of British foreign policy since the Second World War. Winston Churchill had envisaged three concentric circles of post-war British foreign policy. Although they overlapped, each had a distinct emphasis. One concerned relations with the US, another with Europe, and the third with the Commonwealth. The emphasis on the Commonwealth died first.[24] The relationship with Europe has always been problematic. Successive British prime ministers, however, sought a 'special relationship' with the US. Harold Macmillan's relationship with the younger John F. Kennedy was always that of a thoughtful junior, but a junior all the same. Margaret Thatcher sought to elevate the relationship to something that could be at least depicted as one between equals – but that was depiction and not the reality. When President Reagan chose to bomb Libya, British airbases were made available. Efforts at special relationships with Bill Clinton were followed by similar efforts to cultivate the second George Bush. The British prime minister's reasoning in the face of the Bush/Rumsfeld doctrine of international relations would seem to be both pragmatic and optimistically opportunistic:

1. Pragmatic: There is one show in town. It is important to become part of it and to be seen, symbolically at least, as an important and integral part of it.
2. Optimistically opportunistic: What the US is contemplating is incredibly ambitious. Perhaps when it achieves full spectrum it will not be able to hold the line. Even with great technology

it might become overstretched. A leading role must surely then be given to its proven ally and partner. Britain would thereby become again not only a great power, but a great power able to lead Europe, as all the other European powers would have missed or shunned the US boat.

In a sense, but perhaps the British prime minister would miss the historical analogy, what he looked to was a re-run of an overstretched Roman Empire. At the end of the third century, an administration centralized in Rome was no longer able to address threats and issues on all frontiers. A Tetrarchy, a rule of four men in two pairs, was instituted. One pair was meant to guard the west, the other to guard the east. In the end only the east was safeguarded, the Roman Empire relocated its capital to Constantinople (but even then it was far from secure for, in the years leading up to that decision, the Roman Emperor Valerian had been forced to bow in defeat before the Sassanid Persian Emperor, Shapur) and Rome's transition also marked the slow transition of Western civilization from its classical phase to the medieval. There would be no contemplation or expectation of a new medievalism – unless the Islamic complaints of new crusaders is true – but the notion that close alliance with the US might one day result in Britain becoming a Tetrarch is one way of stating the prime minister's not fully articulated ambition.

To be fair to the prime minister, he did seek to persuade Europe to buy into the US doctrine of new international relations, but then he would have been seen as the one who led Europe into the new spectrum. He did seek, more fruitlessly than fruitfully (Dominique de Villepin's speech put paid to that) to retain the UN as both the 'legitimate authority' and a compliant one. Above all, however, he doggedly followed the US ambition to achieve its first great victory – no longer against terror, since Saddam was not anything more than a local tyrant and was certainly not an international terrorist – against a series of geopolitical spaces that espoused defiance, or had espoused defiance, to US hegemony; to issue a warning to all Islamic states – although Iraq, as discussed above, was not a typical Islamic state – that

Islam too had to imbibe liberal values; and to shrink, defiant state by defiant state, the frontiers of defiance.

The states chosen were all in which species of terror, evil, esoteric belief, strangeness and actual dictatorship existed: Iran (despite the visible power struggle there between conservatives and modernizers), perhaps Syria (but this is unlikely for reasons outlined later in this essay) and, venturing beyond Islam and the Middle East, the enigmatic 'Hermit Kingdom' of North Korea (where President Kim Jong Il seems already a replica of every fanciful Hollywood oriental despot). The isolation of the term 'evil' is what makes both the US doctrine and British adherence to it problematic in what has hitherto been a world of secular international relations. Even the diplomats of the Iranian revolution conducted a seamless representation of their state and were admired as the professionals' professionals in Geneva, New York and the great cities of the world. Trumpeting of evil was, in Iran, for local consumption - perhaps seeking wider Islamic solidarity - but it was not a basis for actual foreign policy. If evil was a rhetorical feature of Iranian pronouncements it was in eschatological terms, i.e. the last days were upon the world as signalled by Satanic Western policy, and God would surely overthrow it. The new US and British usage is in soteriological terms, i.e. it is a doctrine of salvation: after evil has been defeated, and we will defeat it, not God, the world will be flooded by democracy and light.

However, the US and its allies are not very good at building democracy and light. The Taliban is regrouping in Afghanistan, as barely reformed warlords from the Mujaheddin era jostle with the bright young technocrats, and win, and do not change their ways beyond fixed, often cosmetic points. The Taliban, after all, had an original message against corruption, and corruption is again rife in Afghanistan. I have already commented on the lack of success and progress in the rebuilding of Iraq - largely devastated by US and British bombs and missiles. Evil has been defeated but, ironically if not tragically, new evils remain. Yet it is the never fully specified and defined, never quite fully articulated and expostulated, but frequently implied, sometimes explicitly stated notion that there is evil and it needs to be overcome that hangs as a backdrop in US discourse, and which is at the heart of the British prime minister's rationale for war. Not holy war - it has been secularized - but *moral* war. It will be time soon in this essay to examine exactly what this evil might or might not be, and whether war against it is moral or not, or whether it is a war of power pretending to be moral.

4 OTHER LANDS AND THE SUPERHAWKS

The fantasy of endless victorious war until the world is sub-dued can only be a fantasy. War is expensive. Just restocking all the cruise missiles fired in the second Gulf War takes time and money. Congress must approve the money and, in effect, approve the wars to come. A future bellicose US president may or may not one day face timid Congresses, and may or may not preside over a US economy able to sustain huge financial outlays. Wars cost lives, and these are of two types. Firstly, US deaths cause doubts among US voters once the numbers rise above a certain level. Secondly, the previously hidden and sanitized deaths of thousands of non-combatants are now broadcast on stations such as Al Jazeera, and the world can see what a just death or a moral death entails. Wars cost alliances. In the second Gulf War there was very little by way of active alliance. Britain, Italy, Spain and Australia supported the US – Britain alone by way of meaningful military participation – and a motley 'coali-tion of the willing' was gerrymandered into the public relations that now go with war: states for the most part with a need to demonstrate support for the US for reasons of their own. The West was split, NATO was split, the European Union was split. The Middle East and the Far East rejected the reasons for war, and Russia was pointedly sceptical. If the US plans full-spectrum dominance as its existential future, then it may be successful in the latter part of that formulation. It is unlikely that even the same British prime minister would wish to weather another US call to arms.

Finally, wars cost credibility. They expose to daily news re-portage the ignorance of US soldiers and the shallowness of plans to meet human concerns. A war against Iraq was won in 21 days. Months later, water, electricity, medicine, law and order, a functioning administration and the restoration of the nation's looted antiquities were not in place. To be fair to those in the frontline trying, they were having to improvise a way forward. The hawks in Washington plan wars but do not, with the same attention to detail and care, plan for the aftermath. Very few US soldiers remain in Afghanistan as that country begins its slide into the anarchy that existed after the departure of the Soviets. For the US to move on to other targets it would have to leave in its wake a trail of unreconstructed states and unconstructed democracies. For the Rumsfeld doctrine depends on the Rumsfeld doctrine actually being able to work: it cannot deploy massively, but has to depend on mobile technology; it cannot be a full-spectrum trudge with massive suitcases from location to location. Despite all this, the gossip, speculation, proto-briefings and think-tank overtimes of Washington are consumed by talk of who or what is next. A great adventure seems under way, built on alarms. A rash of badly argued books, sometimes selling hundreds of thousands, indicate an Islamic threat. In Washington, Islamic states are certainly on the agenda of speculation, and so is North Korea.

War, however, is unlikely to come to Syria, despite fears that Iraqi resistance to the administration in Baghdad is being provisioned via Syria, with the authorities there either turning a blind eye, or elements of the authorities there facilitating the resistance. For, however divided the Syrian regime may be – with a savagely influential rump from the time of President Hafiz Assad who died in 2000 – the new president, Hafiz's son, Bashar Assad, has liberal tendencies. Not enough for now to overturn his father's coterie, but even a US hawk might realize that overthrowing him would be overthrowing a very different character to that of Saddam Hussein. Bashar is not a liberal in the Western mode. He speaks his mind in the time-honoured Ba'th commitment to the Arab cause. The young president very publicly lectured the British prime minister during his visit to Syria, and this was seen in the Arab world as a calculated humiliation. Simultaneously it was a refreshing contrast to the intricate behind-the-scenes manoeuvres of his father, where sweetness and light would be the public face and a knife in the back the common reality. Moreover, there are now 600,000 Syrian users of the internet. That genie means opposition websites that cannot be as easily censored or banned as newspapers and magazines. At some point the Ba'th will have to find an accommodation with criticism, because it will not be able to stop it. Bashar Assad is even said personally to have enjoyed *Addomari* magazine, a brief and persecuted equivalent of *Private Eye* in Britain, *Canard Enchainé* in France, *Feral Tribune* in Croatia and whatever passes for a political satirical magazine in the US.[1] Above all, neither Bashar nor the old guard from the days of Hafiz can do in the region what Hafiz did. Times and conditions have changed, and the fall of the Soviet Union has left Syria without its key ally and international protector. For the Soviet Union, however, its Syrian friend proved to be an individualistic handful. But even that individualism in the last decade of Hafiz Assad supported the first Gulf War against Iraq.

Hafiz Assad rather brilliantly, particularly in the late 1970s and 1980s, exploited the superpower relationship to contrive a role for Syria as a regional power, seeking to balance Israel on Israel's very frontiers. He advanced a doctrine containing what he called three principles. These were, firstly, that an Arab state had a right to intervene militarily in another Arab state in order to protect its own sovereignty. It didn't matter if that traduced the sovereignty of the other state, because the principle from Syria's point of view was that security has a greater value than sovereignty. Secondly, a state could intervene in this manner without seeking permission from either superpower, thus exercising a vocation of regional power. Thirdly, a state regarded as being within the Soviet sphere of influence, e.g. Syria, could intervene in a state regarded as being within the US sphere of influence, e.g. Lebanon, even if this violated the operating principle between the US and Soviet Union that neither intervened in the sphere of the other.[2]

He could only do this – and he did do this by intervening in Lebanon extensively, and did succeed in establishing Syria as a very real balance to the Israeli forward policy at the time – by a series of calculations. He reasoned that the Soviet Union could not find any other regional ally with Syria's strategic value. The Soviet Union needed Syria in its own Cold War calculations, exactly as a balance to US interests as expressed by Israel. This gave Syria some negotiating room and room for manoeuvre with the Soviets, for the Soviets either had to put up with it or install another more compliant regime in Damascus, and this would be messy and costly. Any, even momentary, instability in the region caused by regime change in Syria could open the doors to Islamic fundamentalism, which the secular Ba'th party in Syria was holding at bay. On this basis Hafiz Assad considered that he could intervene in Lebanon: the Soviets would allow it because they did not want to lose Syria as an ally; the US would tolerate it because they did not want to apply any pressure on Syria that would drive her even more deeply into the Soviet embrace. Thus Hafiz manipulated both the Soviet Union and the US.[3] However, he could not have manipulated one without the other. With the demise of the Soviet Union the large Syrian game was also over, whether for Hafiz Assad or his son Bashar. The Syrian old guard, whom Bashar must slowly seek to replace, might not fully know this, but the US should. Victory in the Cold War means that some things do not need to be re-fought in new wars.

However, it is not as if the Syrians retired into a shell. Syria retained a regional policy – it just no longer tried to tweak the noses of superpowers. It long ago ceased supporting acts of international terrorism but has, however, supported militant Islamic Palestinian groups, and a US attack on Syria would see an even more concerted effort by these groups to destabilize Israel. War with Syria would mean greater war within Israel, and even a conservative Israeli administration would not want the US to launch a war so close by and with such immediate knock-on effects. Syria would be swift to remind the US that it participated in the first Gulf War, joining the coalition swiftly. Although it objected to the second Gulf War, it did so alongside all other Arab states; but, as the Arab representative on the UN Security Council, it voted for weapons inspection and agreed to a tough UN diplomatic line.

The Syrian Ba'th, although well known for its history of ruthlessness and its present practice of censorship and repression, is not the same as the Iraqi Ba'th. Until the second Gulf War, when Arab solidarity deemed it in bad taste, Syrian satirists were almost encouraged by the state to lampoon Saddam. His generals were depicted as overfed and greedy, and Saddam himself as vainglorious and stupid. For Saddam, there was no other history possible but Babylon. Syria had had a rich history of Hellenic, post-Hellenic and Roman cross-cultural influences. St Paul's conversion took place on the road to Damascus; the early Christian church had a strong congregation in Antioch; a specific form of Christianity, aligned with Nestorianism and founded by Jacob Baradaeus in the sixth century, flourished in Syria; the Crusader kingdoms were established in Syria; Islam did not persecute the Christian church but the Mongol invaders did; finally the Ottoman Empire came and, with the advent of the British, went. At the height of Islamic expansion in about 750, Syria stood at the very geographical centre of the Islamic world, almost equidistant between the Punjab in the east and the borders of Spain in the west. It abutted the borders of what was left of the Roman legacy in Byzantium and thus was witness to the dawn of medievalism in European history. The Syrian Ba'th was established on pan-Arabism, but it has never doubted the sophistication of Syrian history.

It is thus surely a dictatorship that the US would face, but one in which some liberal change is possible. It is not an Islamic state, but war and destabilization would unleash Islamic forces, just as the second Gulf War unleashed the Shia in Iraq. It is not a crude Arab state founded on a reconstruction of a distant Babylonian past, but one with a continuous international history. Moreover it has access to the sea and has a future as a Mediterranean power as much as an Arab one.

Since the pure Rumsfeld doctrine of technological war proved insufficient in Iraq, and a huge conventional apparatus had to be wheeled into place, the assembly of US forces to attack Syria would be problematic. Iraq could be used as a staging post, but the aim is to get US troops out of Iraq, not put more in, especially as the environment becomes more hostile. Turkey could be used, but Turkey refused facilities for the second Gulf War and would be very conscious that US mobilization on the Turkey/Syria border would be right in the middle of Turkey's own Kurdish zone and all its problems. Jordan could be used, but the new young king would certainly refuse. A huge US presence would only destabilize a finely balanced regime already beset by destabilization in Iraq to its east and the problems of the Israeli/Palestinian stand-off to its west, and facing demands for more transparency and democratization at home. Israel and Lebanon could be used, but Israel would not wish this for the reasons outlined above, and Lebanon is only now recovering from years of war in no small part caused or fuelled by superpower interventions. A maritime invasion from Cyprus would be fanciful. Above all Egypt, the principal US Arab ally, would strongly object, and a longstanding and important alliance would risk being thrown to the winds.

Finally, what would be the cause – the just cause or the moral cause? Syria has given no recent offence, has no unfinished business with the US, and was prepared to defend the US ally, Saudi Arabia, in the first Gulf War. The 'weapons of mass destruction' rubric would not work again, Syria was not at all connected to 9/11 and the Syrian government maintains no links with Al Qaeda. Sympathy for an attack would be hard to garner, an alliance impossible to achieve, and the logistics full of huge difficulties – all in the face of what would be near universal criticism and condemnation.

Not Syria then, but what about the more easily demonized Mullahs of Iran? Outside the Arab zone, seemingly quite convinced, if not manifestly so, of its own 'civilizational' difference and opposition to the West, it was the very font of 'something new' in international relations, awkwardly setting itself into place a decade before the end of history, but thankfully contained for the better part of that decade by Iraq.

The end of history Iranian style

The assumption behind an application of Hegel, as universal philosophy, to a statement of universal history – history has come to the end of its possible progress on Western terms – is that this is a unique as well as universal statement. The imagination of other universal philosophy and its application to ideas of another universal history is not a key variable. If there is the possibility of a variable, then what Western history has accomplished will be defended, the variables treated as challenges and rolled back.

Fukuyama, in the book of the article, did speculate on a new 'first man' restarting history, but this was almost an abstract warning. The new men of *thymos* alone, precisely because they were composed of *thymos*, would not have a universal philosophy. Fukuyama, in short, did not look into the question of actual alternative philosophies, alternative histories and alternative conceptions of the 'first man'.

Moreover, there is a fundamental problem of extra-rationality when one looks at the work of Hegel and Nietzsche. When Hegel speaks of a Spirit of History he is using an image, a metaphor, and in one of his prefaces – not always translated for the English editions – he likens the Spirit of History to God's Holy Ghost, i.e. he explains his metaphor by reference to another metaphor: history's animating and progressive capacity is like the power or agency God uses to animate and direct the progress of creation. There is not *actually* a Spirit of History. Although the sense of progressive history, of progress in itself, is part of the Enlightenment heritage, the image of an almost sentient History is metaphysical and romantic. If this is the mixed heritage of Hegel, then Nietzsche is more fully romantic. Zarathustra, Nietzsche's rendition of the Persian philosopher and spiritual leader, Zoroaster, seeks fulfilment and the sense that humanity has a capacity for fulfilment, via a series of adventures and encounters that are moral fables containing characters who are necessarily one-dimensional – caricatures – and who are finally comic and failed creatures as Zarathustra continues what becomes, like any quest tale, a romanticized search for something others don't have. For Fukuyama to use Hegel and Nietzsche he would have to employ philosophical devices that are suggestive, imagistic, powerful but not precise. The notion of perfectibility, however, – the perfect prophet (or prophets), the perfect teaching and the perfect history of a perfectible world – is not unique to Western thought.

The Iranian revolution became dominated by clerics who had both an anti-version and a similar version to what I have described above. It was an anti-version in that it lacked the idea of linear progress. Indeed it looked backwards, not forwards, to a time when the bedrock personality of Shia belief – which sepa-

rates it from Sunni Islam – the Twelfth Imam, the direct descendant of Mohammed, achieved 'occultation', i.e. he withdrew
from the world (about 874) and became the 'hidden Imam',
destined to appear again at the end of history. At that time he
will fill the world with justice. History, in short, will end with the
appearance not of 'first men', but of just men. Looking backwards in this manner provided a springboard to look, quite
suddenly, with history as a gap to be crossed, to the future moment of justice.[4]

The interesting, almost ironic twist here is that, in late twentieth-century history, there were different versions of something
coming to an end and something new either beginning or con-
solidating. The Iranian version is in many ways, at this point,
more progressive. The Western version has history coming to an
end, satisfied with itself and its accomplishments, guarding itself
perhaps against 'first men' who might seek to restart history.
History becomes fulfilled, having won the world, but becomes
conservative. The Iranian version has history just beginning to
make decisive progress, for the reappeared Imam will change the
world. Both versions contain idealisms and romanticisms. Neither has a scientific foundation. Both Fukuyama's US and the
Iran of the victorious Imams entered the twenty-first century with
faith on their side – metaphysical, metaphorical, spiritual, religious, one or more of these – and the US view of Iran had better
be quite differently based than its view of Iraq.

As for Iraq, its war with Iran effectively removed any widespread Iranian 'threat' to the world. Iranian rhetoric certainly
radicalized and supported many regional causes. It armed and
supported the Shia in Lebanon, and it sought to make militant
the *Hajj*, the religious pilgrimage to Mecca, seeking to turn it into
a denunciation of Saudi Arabia's growing affiliation to the West.
However, its influence was constricted by the need to concen-
trate on the Iraqi threat. Saddam certainly had in mind the
diminution of Iranian influence in the Persian Gulf. It has been
observed that many of the smaller Gulf states had welcomed the
Iranian presence there, precisely as a balance to the ambitions of
larger states such as Iraq.[5] During the first decade of the Iranian
revolution, and while at war with Iraq, rhetoric against the US

was at its height. The embassy hostages affair and the abortive
attempt by President Carter to rescue the hostages inflamed
emotions on both sides. The sense that the US and other Western powers were economically facilitating Iraq's drive into Iran
certainly did not help diminish the fire in Iranian pronouncements. Philip G. Philip, however, sees all of this as part of a
deliberate and short-term policy:

> It may be argued that revolutionary Iran faced some of the most
> powerful states in a nuclear world and, given the circumstances it
> found itself to be in, imposed its dictate for what seems to be specific
> short-term goals, such as achieving the reputation of a defiant mid-
> dle power while finally shrugging off the yoke of centuries of foreign
> interference and domination.[6]

Moreover, as mentioned earlier in this essay, Iran's confrontation with the US was not based purely on an Islamic world view,
but one that mixed Islam with a Third Worldism. Ayatollah
Khomeini may have spoken of the 'path of God' on the one
hand, and the 'path of Satan' on the other, but he also spoke of
the *mostazafin*, those who lack power and who are oppressed, and
the *mustakbarin*, those who oppress and have the power to do so.[7]
Certainly by the end of the war with Iraq, many Iranian academics at least believed that the conceptual task facing Iran was to
make congruent 'divine norms and laws with the conventional
interpretations of nationality in the contemporary international
system'.[8]

Despite the bloodiness, purges and deaths - indeed, the
internal oppression - of the Iranian revolution, it had to struggle
from the very beginning with a form of congruence between
divine laws and conventional ones. This was as pronounced at
home as abroad. What was meant to be an 'Islamic' constitution
is a case in point. This was first formulated in 1979, but has had
to have exceptional clauses added to it since, and was meant to
enshrine the notion of law held by the victorious clerics. Bearing
in mind that Sharia law was derived from sacred precepts, that
the concept of *aqida wa sharia* meant that belief and law could
not in any case be divided, that the concept of *din wa dawla*
meant a union of state and religion, and that *din wa dunya* stood
for the essential unity of both spiritual and secular values, it

would appear that an Islamic constitution would ensure a clerical interpretation of all life, and indeed many hardline clerics intended just that. However, to do that comprehensively would have meant amassing, often writing from scratch, a huge body of law related to petty but modern problems of life. For instance, it would have meant a clerical and scriptural determination of laws on motor traffic, which could have had no possible emanation from either the Koran or Sharia. Slight as this exception might seem, the large number of such exemptions meant the possibility of some juristic debate, in which purely secular considerations would have to be contemplated. More importantly, however, there was an existing and fundamental (not fundamentalist) Islamic precept to do with emergencies. 'Emergencies make it permissible to do what is forbidden', provided there was no original desire to do what was forbidden.[9] The juristic debate would, under this rubric, permit at least the contention that 'emergency' would include conditions of compulsion, distress and disadvantage. Since these may be subjectively felt, the element of an individual right is instantly introduced.

Such individual rights are not automatically those of the West. As outlined earlier in this essay, there are centuries of Islamic thought and debate concerning God as a 'necessary existent' and each person merely as a 'contingent existent'. However, even though we exist dependently on God, this same God wishes for our welfare and does not wish us to enter harm or incur wilful self-harm. God recognizes our existence is contingent on other matters and persons than Himself alone, and accords us the right of self-protection in the face of oppressive circumstances. In juristic debate, these may be formulated as 'emergencies'.

More than that, Iran is largely but not entirely Shia. There are large Ismaili and Sufi populations, each but particularly the latter concerned with the mystical concept of individual union with God. They are, as it were, the 'charismatics' of Islam. None of this, even in Iran, exists in an insulated enclave – communities and beliefs do influence one another. What this means is that there is a Sufi sense of autonomy, i.e. that one must realize and perfect oneself as a precondition to realizing oneself in union with God, that is qualitatively different to, and acts as a qualifying sense to a pure notion of dependency and contingency. The idea of agency therefore could not be obliterated by the clerics, nor the idea of a right to resistance to oppression, and certainly not the idea that matters of traffic law, international trade, membership of the UN and a myriad other things did not depend on prescriptive instruction from Sharia alone. This is why the 'Islamic' constitution had to keep having secular exceptions added to it. The constitution and the conditions of complex daily life provide sufficient ambivalence for the political struggle between reformers (including progressive clerics) and conservative clerics to be based on precisely this inescapable ambivalence.

It is also important to remember that the revolution, in the first instance, was an alliance between secular reformers and clerics. Although Foucault said it was 'something new', Fred Halliday has been more precise in exactly why this revolution was 'modern' but the Russian and Chinese ones were not. It was largely an urban revolution, and it involved people from almost every walk of urban life, and they came from a society with an advanced socio-economic system. It was not a 'Third World' revolution of peasants and the dispossessed. The revolutionaries were the products of an education system and had a per capita income in the 1970s of US$2,000.[10] Among the ambitions they shared was a revulsion towards the regime of the Shah, with all its oppressive apparatus, and the fact that this regime was so strongly supported by the US. Even though the clerical faction came to monopolize the revolution, and even though moderates and reformers are even now struggling with them for a greater liberalism and political freedom, it is not as if all those who are outside the clerical camp are supporters of the West. It is not a situation where, if the conservative clerics fell tomorrow, the US would have an instant ally – just as the overthrown regime of Saddam has not produced an Iraq in love with its liberators. Perhaps – but this is certainly for now speculation – if the US invaded Iran, as it did Iraq, reformers and conservatives alike would stand and resist.

And it is not as if Iran's history is nothing but Islamic, and that nothing exists in the equation but Islam and the West.

There is a very proud pre-Islamic history in which Persia – as it was then called – was a world superpower. There is an eleventh-century epic poem, with proportions and ambitions somewhat greater than the *Iliad*, and with characters every bit as wilful and tragic, called *The Epic of the Kings*.[11] Although Persia was by then within Islam, this epic harks back to a time of Zoroastrian kings, and it sets out to counterpoint the national (the Persian) with the international. This established a tradition within Persian and Islamic literature which has been continuous. In the case of *The Epic of the Kings*, an ambivalence is established between the national and the international, but it is the national that emerges superior. Part of the epic concerns the wars between the Romans and Persians. The era of Pompey is retold through Persian eyes, as is the period of some 200 years when the two empires sought to establish borders of benefit to their ambitions and senses of themselves. What is striking, however, is how cosmopolitan the Persian account is. In one chapter alone (XXXIV), the cast of characters and events include the Persian ruler, the Roman Caesar, the Khan of China, four Greek philosophers, a Christian city, a debate on Hinduism, plus a Roman princess and 40 Greek eunuchs 'who captivated the heart'. But the highlight is when a Zoroastrian philosopher lectures the Roman Caesar on Christianity, defending the merits of Christ, and the lecture is rewarded with Roman approval. A Persian emperor could not only defeat a Caesar, as Shapur did defeat Valerian, but a Persian philosopher could teach a Caesar. There is still, in Iran today, that sense that it is not only the West that has something to say.

If the US decides to move against Iran it would be moving not just against 'fundamentalist' clerics but a highly sophisticated nation of vast cosmopolitan history. But why move in any case, if the case is to spread democracy? There is already a struggle for political liberalism and greater democracy in Iran that needs no US help, but would be jeopardized by US sabre-rattling and the ammunition against dissent it would give the clerics in their last stands.

The US might, however, be tempted to move on the grounds that Iran was developing a nuclear bomb. The International Atomic Energy Agency has had difficulties mounting proper inspections of Iran's civilian nuclear facilities, particularly after the second Gulf War. Traces of weapons-grade uranium have been found at one such facility at Natanz. How developed or primitive any Iranian bomb programme is at this stage is unknown. We do not have any sense of an Iranian nuclear doctrine, although given events in Iraq, both when Saddam Hussein went to war against Iran, and with the US now posturing from Iraq, deterrence might be a reasonable bet. The thing is, Iran has never attacked anyone in its revolutionary history. Nor would any bomb be the dreaded 'Islamic bomb', since the isolation of the Shia regime is manifold – the Shia being the minority party in international Islam, and the Iranian clerics being highly introspective. It would not be the 'Islamic bomb' any more than Pakistan's is. But US sabre-rattling on this particular issue would indeed strengthen the hands of the clerical conservatives. The US has, however, other putatively nuclear issues on its mind.

Shapur's defeat of Valerian took place 1,700 years ago. In its search for states to occupy, the US has identified one candidate who, only half a century ago – and unlike Afghanistan and Iraq – fought the US to a standstill. In North Korea the version of history is that the US was defeated. And it was not a defeat by guerrilla war, or of a government the US had installed then left behind; it was in a war of appalling full-frontal charges and conventional exchanges of the most bloody ferocity, in which the US General Douglas MacArthur sought permission to use atomic weapons, since his troops could not hold out except with extreme difficulty.

The hermit kingdom

North Korea is an enigma even in the Far East. Under the Shogunate, the Japanese devised belittling names for the Koreans, calling them 'garlic eaters' on account of their diet and their breath. There is a somewhat crude joke that one thing unites the Chinese and Japanese, and that is their shared opinion on what an odd and primitive lot the Koreans are. None of this is deserved – except that kim chee is indeed a somewhat fiery mixture of cabbage, chilli and garlic – and some of it is probably due to an earlier history when Korea devised its own system of writing and broke away from the Chinese characters still used today by both the Chinese and Japanese. The Koreans themselves trace their descent through a rich history. The earliest historical records, the *samguk sagi* (Records of the Three Kingdoms) and *samguk yusa* (Stories of the Three Kingdoms), date only from the twelfth century, but they recount dynasties that ruled as far back as the third century. The Silla, Paekche and Koguryo kingdoms emerge in these histories from the mists of time, and are portrayed as centres of great culture and civilization. Some of this is certainly corroborated by tomb excavations. As for the primeval mists of time, Korea was apparently founded by a shaman-king, Tangun, also known as the Sandalwood Prince, who was descended from God via a bear-woman. The legacy of Tangun was an ingrained shamanism in Korean spiritual life, only officially superseded by Confucianism (in the Silla dynasty from about 600) and Buddhism. Christianity gained significant support from the eighteenth century onwards. Despite the advent of formal church-based practice, shamanic influences remained and found a cloak in the spread of Taoism. As elsewhere, Taoism forged syncretic links with other religions, but the mystical quality of Korean belief, combining spiritual worlds and crossovers between the animal and human worlds, is quite unique in the Far East. Korea became known as the 'Hermit Kingdom', somewhat outside the mainstream.

This would simply be colourful narrative but for two things not often observed. The first is that archaeological evidence of kingdoms such as Silla and Paekche is concentrated in what is now South Korea. The North Korean ambition for a union of the entire nation is not only political but nostalgic, seeking to include those sites that validate the Korean nation. The second is that the partly invented but hugely exaggerated legends spun around the North Korean leaders are not merely Stalinist vainglories but derive in their narrative structure from very ancient tales of magical kings in magical kingdoms.[12]

Heavily invested in such legendary qualities, the first North Korean leader, Kim Il Sung – the 'Iron-Clad Commander' in his ruder propaganda – presented a striking figure to Western commentators.[13] Although a tendency arose among them to dismiss all Kim's achievements and heroics as propaganda and pomposity, there is some foundation to his claims to have been an anti-Japanese fighter – and this, curiously, was on the Allied side. The Japanese had occupied Korea from 1910 to 1945, and their reign was very frequently cruel. Korean women were shipped to the Japanese lines in the Second World War as 'comfort women' for the soldiers. Exemplary executions, including those on a mass scale, occurred. Korean culture was discouraged and sometimes suppressed. It is probably no surprise that after the war the re-invention of Korean culture involved much attention to the invigoration of a martial art called Tae Kwon Do, and the North Korean version has named all the formal exercises after episodes of resistance to the Japanese.

During the war, however, Korean resistance could only be headquartered outside the country – repression within being too strong. Kim Il Sung emerged first as a fighter with a Chinese unit and, from 1940, as a captain in a Soviet-led offensive against the Japanese. In 1937 he had won a significant military victory at the battle of Pochonbo, and this catapulted his identity into the wider Korean imagination. His rise to political power, however, owed much to Soviet support and, precisely because the Cold War began so soon after the Second World War, Korea was divided at the 38th parallel with Kim Il Sung's Democratic People's Republic of Korea to the north. But the Cold War, although cold elsewhere, flared into red hot violence in Korea. Almost all US strategic debate since 1950 to the present day has been influenced by those events in Korea.

The early days of North Korea were full of rhetoric, condemnation of imperialism and calls for reunification with the south. Simultaneously there were discernible elements of pragmatism in its foreign policy. An application to join the United Nations was lodged in 1949, but this was as the sole representative of both North and South. The UN, with US steerage, rejected the application. The North Korean manoeuvre had been, however, as much about hamfisted diplomacy – seeking to combine two objectives in one irreconcilable package – as anything else. The desire to be a member of the UN, in one way or another, was probably real. The desire for reunification was very real, and it seemed that the US in particular was intent on preventing this.

Thereafter North Korea looked to a solution to its problems by force, and on the evening of 25 June 1950 its forces crossed the 38th parallel and war began. It was to be a very bitter war, led by US forces under UN colours (the Security Council vote took place in the absence of the Soviet representative who had stormed out of the debate), but with a dominant US command structure. Although later commentators judged the conflict to have been a 'limited war',[14] or to have been a war that 'remained manageable', i.e. one in which the adversaries had not become 'prisoners of a chain of events which neither of them foresaw and none controls',[15] this was very close to not being the case.

In October 1950 US forces won a major victory at Inchon, not far from Seoul and also not far from the border. Thereafter US troops stormed across the 38th parallel, no longer intent on restoring the situation to the *status quo ante* - the remit of the UN Security Council resolution - but intent on taking the north as well. Their advances made huge inroads into North Korean territory and headed towards the Yalu River, the Chinese border in Manchuria. The rest of that war, until its end in 1953, saw massive Chinese intervention on the side of the North Koreans, the forcing back of US forces, General MacArthur's desire to use atomic weapons to turn the tide back in the US favour, and protracted and difficult negotiations that finally restored both sides to where they had been before - divided at the 38th parallel.

The war had many long-term consequences, not least the continued division of Korea. One legacy was 'prolonged American hostility towards the People's Republic of China: for twenty years Washington blocked the admission of the Communist government of China to the UN seat occupied by the Nationalist regime on Taiwan.'[16] This hostility only ended with the Kissinger/Nixon approach to China almost two decades later. More importantly, however, the war greatly influenced debate on strategic doctrine in the US. I summarize this below. It also, in a less appreciated way, determined strategic doctrine in North Korea. If it comes to war between these two again, each may, or may not, have learnt much from the last time.

In the US there is a view that public reaction to the war was such that a deliberate search for non-nuclear or, more specifi-cally, controlled-nuclear doctrine was engendered. This was to avoid mass nuclear destruction in the event that nuclear-armed adversaries were drawn into what had been smaller conflicts.[17] If this is true it had to develop as a doctrine slowly, as the Dulles doctrine of massive retaliation held sway for a decade after the Korean War. Indeed, what Dulles was saying was that there would be no more Koreas, or at least no more Koreas with US troops fighting across hostile territory. Provocation would be met not by troops but by nuclear bombs. Whether outright nuclear or controlled nuclear, there had been in Washington a feeling that Korea, notwithstanding its strategic insignificance – Secretary of State Dean Acheson had described South Korea as being outside the perimeter of major US defence interests – nevertheless presented a challenge to the US and the West precisely because they previously had allowed 'insignificant' countries to be over-run by powers that went on to pose a confident challenge to the US and the West: Japan against Manchuria in 1931, Japan against what was still Nationalist China in 1937, German acts of aggression in Europe in 1938 and 1939, and the very recent Communist triumph over Nationalists in China itself.[18] The feeling was that at some point – and that point was now – an evil had to be confronted and rolled back.

It was the extent of rolling back that concerned many. Had the US forces driven the North Koreans back to the 38th paral-lel, both the UN and a cautiously approving US Congress would have been satisfied and have had no cause for complaint. The decision to go beyond the 38th parallel, to take the fight to the enemy, to march on his capital with the intent of regime change, seemed to be less like rolling back and more like conquest, less like confronting and controlling an enemy and more like punish-ing him and achieving victory over him. Although Michael Walzer sees a degree of plain military hubris in MacArthur's determination to overthrow the north, he also advances an analysis that is concerned with a utilitarian proportionality: what greater good was accomplished by the greater cost of exceeding the 38th parallel?[19] Walzer cites a line from Shakespeare's *Troilus and Cressida*: "Tis mad idolatry to make the service greater than the god.' He also cites a line from the British First World War strategic thinker Basil Liddell Hart: 'The object in war is a better state of peace.' Walzer reminds us that the key word is 'better'. It is not 'perfect'. War, in short, is more easily described as just if it is also limited. It corrects a wrong. But it is driven neither by hubris nor by the sense of perfectibility. War cannot be ideological and just.

What we see, however, in today's War on Evil is precisely a Rumsfeld sense of military superiority that may yet be leading in the peace-free Iraq to hubris, and a sense not of massive retaliation – for there was no offence against the US – but of massive intervention on the grounds not of correcting a wrong – that was the effect of the first Gulf War – but of the need to tame a region on behalf of a vision of the world that is both idealistic and US-centric. But what of the North Korean vision of the world? This may or may not be idealistic. It may certainly be perverse. It may certainly be used to justify great cruelty and ruthlessness to its own people. But it may also be Korean-centric, imbued with a mystical sense that it also has been chosen, alone, to stand against the forces of evil.

After the end of the 1950–53 war, watching the funds the US and other Western states were pouring into South Korea, and wary of being incorporated into either a Soviet or a Chinese Communist zone but desperately needing development all the same, North Korea embarked upon an assiduous self-reliance campaign called *juche*. Huge posters and billboards sprang up everywhere exhorting people to 'go forward with the *juche* idea', following the direction pointed out by a towering figure of Kim Il Sung on each of these billboards, depicted now as a smiling demi-god of infallible proportions. It was in a way monstrous, and the *juche* programme was far from an unbridled success.[20] It did not have the catastrophic backlash of China's Great Leap Forward, but it did depend on the development of heavy industry from a very low base. Soviet funds helped keep the programme on the road, and it must be said that by the 1970s North Korea had achieved a strong, if static, industrial base and a capacious cradle-to-grave welfare system. Third World delegations were uniformly staggered by the extent of social provision. But it was also a police state of immense intrusion into daily life, and deliberate isolation of the population allowed the leadership to cultivate the popular belief that North Korea alone was a workers' paradise without the depredations of the capitalist West and the immiseration of the Third World. Even now, amidst famine and with their industrial base long rendered obsolete in an electronic world, North Koreans evince a faith in their country and their leaders. This might be, of course, the product of isolation and ignorance and of the ruthless repression of other world views. It might also be, in part, the result of recent historical pride in a period when self-reliance seemed to work and benefits could be both seen and felt.

It was, however, the application of self-reliance to defence policy and particularly to nuclear doctrine that alarmed the US. From the North Korean point of view, General MacArthur had wanted to drop atomic bombs on the north. It would have been the only country bombed with such weapons apart from Japan. After 1953 the US established a considerable nuclear arsenal in the south so that in the north the nuclear threat has been constant and it has not had a deterrent weapon of its own. From the US point of view, North Korean policy has been trigger-happy: the seizure of the US frigate *Pueblo* after it strayed into North Korean waters in 1968, the shooting down of a US plane in 1969, leaving 31 people dead, the assassination of several South Korean ministers visiting Burma in 1983, and the shooting down of a South Korean airliner in 1987 – all this suggested a defence doctrine that contained the belligerence of an aggressive power. After the 1969 incident, in which the US plane had been downed, it was said that Kissinger and Nixon played with the idea of dropping a nuclear bomb on the north.[21] Whether this was true or not, the north certainly heard the rumours, which fed into a vicious spiral, with both sides increasingly distrustful of the other, and both contemplating either the use or the development of nuclear weapons.

The development and doctrine of the hermit bomb

The history of the North Korean bomb became more than an abstract aspiration with the end of the Cold War. Without a

Soviet Union to balance the US and befriend North Korea, the north was left to face the West alone. It could afford no more trigger-happy incidents, but it was still deeply concerned about the US military presence in the south – sure that this presence contained a nuclear capacity and acutely conscious of possessing neither military allies nor its own deterrent. If it came to conventional war, the north was certain that its highly drilled forces would win. In order to dissuade the north from that conviction, the US had for years conducted military exercises with the South Koreans under the operational title of 'Team Spirit'. Nevertheless the end of the Cold War did lead to substantial pragmatism on the part of the north. Both North and South Korea agreed to apply for UN membership separately in 1991. To assuage the anxiety related to reunification, talks on the subject became more flexible and led to substantial progress – at least in the realm of measurable gestures – between 1990 and 1992. Both North and South Korea agreed on the need to de-nuclearize the entire country. Even the 'Team Spirit' exercises were called off for 1992. In 1993, however, 'Team Spirit' resumed. The North Koreans were incensed, seeing this as a repudiation of all the recent progress made and also of its effort at pragmatism. Kim Jong Il, the son of the ailing Kim Il Sung and now president-designate, placed the north on a war footing.

The US for its part was intent on using 'Team Spirit' not as a preparation for war but as a sign that it was not satisfied with North Korea's much rumoured effort to develop nuclear weapons, despite progress in talks with the south. The suspicion was that the north was trying to have it both ways: to de-nuclearize the US presence while nuclearizing itself. North Korea had failed to sign the Nuclear Safeguards Agreement (a protocol of the Nuclear Non-Proliferation Treaty, which North Korea had indeed signed in 1985). After a bitter exchange of words, and another botched diplomatic effort to link signature of the NSA with US de-nuclearization in the south, the north had finally signed the agreement in April 1992. But six inspections by the International Atomic Energy Agency from that time to March 1993 had led to such suspicions and recriminations – the north complaining that the IAEA was intrusive and an instrument of the US - that North Korea threatened to pull out of the Nuclear Non-Proliferation Treaty entirely. It was in this context that 'Team Spirit' resumed. The north, for its part, announced it was on a permanent war alert.

The postures, efforts at improving relations, breakdowns because of real or imagined threats or simple cultural clumsiness, have continued for a decade. In all that time, whether it has been making its best efforts or not, North Korea does not seem to have developed an arsenal of nuclear bombs. It has experimented with missile systems - much to the dismay of Japan - but does not seem to have a bank of such missiles. It is certainly the case that, with the accession to the presidency of Kim Jong Il following the death of Kim Il Sung, a brash stridency coupled with what must be called an appallingly developed brattishness has infused North Korean rhetoric and diplomacy. The tone is no longer wild yet picturesque, extreme yet rooted in historical symbolisms, socialist-realist yet enigmatic, antique and isolated because of both historical inclination and contemporary choice. Kim Jong Il grew up in pampered luxury, he has fought no wars as an 'Iron-Clad Commander', he has forged no nation based on *juche* and he has no experience even of working with military units of different countries, as Kim Il Sung had with units from China and the Soviet Union. China is as bewildered by his pronouncements and manoeuvres as everyone else, and the Soviet Union doesn't exist any more. Kim Jong Il is an anachronism by inheritance and his own will. The son, however, is as strong willed as the father. Does the spoilt and strong-willed president of the Hermit Kingdom have a rationale or doctrine for the bomb he boasts he has developed but may still be seeking to make? Few could really answer this question. What is sketched below is only a possible answer. It is based, however, on a North Korean commitment to progress that never took itself substantially beyond the paradigms of industrialization - and of defence doctrine - that infused the rest of the world in the middle era of the twentieth century. Those paradigms should be seen in the context of recent history - with what are felt to be victories over the Japanese and, more importantly, the US - and ancient history's account of the origins of the Korean people.

Alone, of all the Iraqs, Irans and Syrias of the world, the North Koreans could develop *and* deploy nuclear weapons capable of reaching targets at the outermost edges of their region. Even if all these countries had nuclear weapons, North Korea may well, if pressed hard, be most ready to use them. I do use the term 'if pressed hard', because I do not think that North Korea would unilaterally engage in nuclear warfare. It would not seek to nuclear bomb the south, precisely because it cherishes reunification with the south - and this does not mean a destroyed south. The North Koreans could never manufacture missiles of sufficient range to threaten the US, nor could they manufacture enough nuclear bombs or warheads to cause large-scale 'insensate destruction' on any adversary.

The North Korean possession of nuclear weapons would be a deterrent against the US, and this would be on two bases. Firstly, although outgunned by the US in terms of nuclear capacity, North Korea would seek to make it disproportionately costly for the US to invade the north, either by conventional or nuclear forces. Secondly, although it could not cause 'insensate destruction' on the US, it could cause something of this kind on parts of Japan - Kobe and then Tokyo might well become targets. The order of targeting I have suggested would be within a North Korean adaptation of a Herman Kahn scenario - by sending a signal to the US via retaliation upon an ally: 'Stop now, or it will be Tokyo next.' Of course the very possibility of such a strategy would help persuade Japan to object strongly to any US attack on North Korea.

Scenarios of this sort are exactly what prompt the hawks in Washington to toy with the idea of attacking North Korea in the very near future, before it gains operational nuclear capacity. And, in the war of words and symbols, North Korea has now left the Non-Proliferation Treaty. But even if North Korea could only defend itself by conventional means, it would likely defend itself ferociously. It views its history as one in which it defeated first the Japanese, then the US itself. It does not even need the chain of association that briefly sustained the Taliban - that it had defeated the Soviet Union in the same year as Communism began to fall apart, and, having 'defeated' one superpower so comprehensively, it would surely defeat the other. North Korea has an inflated but significantly real history of having engaged the US directly and – even though it was with massive Chinese help, which would not again be available – rolled the US back. The north would be certain it could do so again, and its mountainous terrain would not allow the US to operate unopposed against vast tracts of desert as was the case in Iraq.

The great archaeological remains of the fabled Silla and Paekche kingdoms are at the extreme end of South Korea. North Korea contains within its borders only one truly significant religious and mystical site, and that is Mt Kumgangsan, which was sacred to the early shamans. Even now there are residual shamans, *mudang*, who are possessed by spirits and thus make themselves available for human petition to the spiritual world. The idea of a mediator between heaven and earth, with the earthly strength of a mountain bear and the wisdom of a heavenly omniscient, is what has lain as the background representation of a huge number of ostensibly socialist-realist posters and billboards of Kim Il Sung and, less convincingly, of Kim Jong Il. Nevertheless Kim Jong Il remains the leader of a nation in which belief in him, in the North Korean effort at self-reliance, in reunification and in defiance of the ambitions of the US – despite all manner of repressions and disasters – is strong. He may not be the son of a bear-woman, but he is the son of a man who stamped himself upon the North Korean psyche. If the US comes it will face great resistance, and the last hermits of the world will call upon their ancient spirits and fight. The US will have to come in force and in-depth; it cannot hope for a clean and sharp technological 'shock and awe'. It would be precisely as it mobilizes to come, before it is even in place, that North Korea would strike for Seoul and possibly Japan. Even when the US eventually wins, the carnage will have been such that revulsion will drive the hawks from power.

✠ ✠ ✠ ✠ ✠

If the US, in the early-century dream of the hawks, does wage war on North Korea, or on Iran, perhaps even on Syria, what would be gained? If it is to be a just war, what is to be gained must be articulated in limited terms, for a just war is a limited war. There would seem to be no limited objectives in any case that would justify war. A war against North Korea could hardly be limited, either in objectives or conduct. Bloody regime change would be the very wide aim. Then it would have to be articulated as a moral war against a regime so immoral that its evil imprint could no longer be tolerated upon the earth. But what is this evil? In neither the North Korean nor Iranian case has any attack been launched against the US. No recent significant terrorism has emanated from these countries against the US or its Western allies. Neither country hosts or maintains contact with Al Qaeda. If it is not a case of operational evil, i.e. of evil directed outwards, is there a case to be made about the especial quality of evil that is practised within? Is, for instance, the North Korean regime at this point in time so despicably evil that the world is contaminated? Or is the world likely to be contaminated? Or is it really a hermit kingdom, isolated and isolable, anxious to arm itself but not for reasons of attacking others? Do we have here cases that are actually enigmatic and strange, hard to understand and predict, unable to be fed into computer programs that calculate activity and response? Is it that we fear a future with the North Koreas of the world both because of our own memories of a past in which we shed disproportionate blood in a strange land, and because we have maintained an ignorance of what might underlie the strangeness? The North Korean case is almost tragi-comic, rather than a threat to world peace, and those with the greatest stakes in a regional peace, China and Japan, do not want war with North Korea. Not even South Korea wants to see a re-run, probably much bloodier this time, of 1950-53. And if the North Korean bomb, whether real, planned, imminent or fantastic, is indeed for deterrence and self-defence, what is happening here? It is the US that has been sabre-rattling, not the North Koreans.

Perhaps it might be appropriate to conclude this part of my essay with a passage from the Iranian literary work, *The Epic of the Kings*, to which I referred earlier. I said that an Iranian philosopher delivered a lecture to Caesar, the ruler of the West, on the merits of Christ. The lecture was not only about the moral qualities of Christ but about the countervailing qualities of evil that were inimical to those of Christ, and were qualities the Caesar had adopted:

> Do you not see what Jesus son of Mary said when he was revealing the secrets which had been hidden? He said, If someone takes your shirt, do not contend too fiercely with him, and if he smites you on the cheek so that your vision darkens because of the blow, do not put yourself into a rage nor let your face turn pale. Close your eyes to him and speak no harsh word. In your eating be content with the least morsel of food, and if you lack worldly possessions do not seek about after them. Overlook the evil things and pass meekly through this dark vale. But for you now lust has become dominant over wisdom and your hearts have gone astray from justice and honour. Your palaces soar up to Saturn and camels are needed to carry the keys to your treasure-houses. With the treasures you have arrayed many armies in resplendent proud armour. Everywhere you fight as aggressors, destroy the peace with your swords, and turn the fields into pools of blood. The messiah did not guide you along this path.[22]

Perhaps, amidst the din of sabres rattling, someone from the East is seeking to say something similar, at the dawn of the new millennium, to hawks and governments in the West.

PART III

OUT OF EVIL

5 THE VEIL OF GOOD

In the Biblical tale the corollary of knowing good and evil is also knowing when you are wearing no clothes. In the more recent fairytale, the emperor who didn't know he was naked revealed his lack of discernment as much as his physical appara- tus. Is what the US seeks to accomplish in the world a true championship of good over evil, or is there naked ambition at work? There are a number of factors that must go into the mix of either championship or naked ambition.

1. 9/11 was a true shock to the US and it resorted to a War on Terror without knowing how to conduct such a war.
2. The first stage of this war found terror, rather conveniently, accommodated in a single geopolitical entity, Afghanistan, and so war was pressed upon Afghanistan. This suited military planners, who did not know how to fight a shadowy interna- tional opponent but did know how to fight a national army.
3. The precedent and relative success of the Afghanistan venture meant a War on Terror by successive stages – country by country – so the search was on for a list of suitable countries, and this list was given the soundbite name, the Axis of Evil. The war was a War on Evil.
4. Although considerations of oil wealth have loomed large from the beginning, even in Afghanistan,[1] certainly in Iraq, it would not seem that oil is a primary consideration for US planners. North Korea, for instance, is not an oil-rich country. Rather, oil becomes an important but incidental benefit of 'full-spectrum dominance' – in which the US is unrivalled in all geostrategic and possibly geoeconomic parts of the world.
5. This 'full-spectrum dominance' was to have been occasioned by state-of-the-art military technology, capable of 'shock and awe' devastation. The initial bunglings in the Iraq military

operation were partly caused by debate within the US administration, between Defense Secretary Rumsfeld and the
Pentagon generals, the latter knowing that men on the
ground plus extensive support networks were indispensable in
any conventional war. The cost of such conventional apparatus, and the huge cost of securing peace after having won the
war, may cast doubt on the longevity of this current phase of
'full-spectrum dominance'.

6. This current phase is, however, one in an historical line. Its
post-war template was John Foster Dulles's doctrine of massive retaliation, using technological weaponry that opponents
did not yet possess, and pressing home that advantage to
dominate the world. It was an effort at unipolar international
relations. President Reagan, in instituting what many analysts
have called a 'Second Cold War',[2] was concerned about the
possibility of maintaining an equilibrium between the two superpowers proper, but defeating the Soviet Union in all its
Third World outposts, i.e. the US would dominate all the
world that was not the Soviet Union. The notion of 'Star
Wars'-style defensive shields against nuclear attack, slashing
the usefulness of deterrent missiles in any country that did
not have such a shield, was an effort again to establish an unanswerable technological dominance in the world at large and
dominate strategically even the Soviet Union. The fall of the
Soviet Union allowed, near the end of the millennium, the
possibility once again of a unipolar world.

7. This is to see the march of contemporary history purely
through competitive lenses: one is attacked, one must respond; one may be attacked, one must be prepared to
respond; the competition is in the capacity to have the highest
grade of response, so that attack will not take place. The attack of 9/11, apart from being the first actual attack upon the
US mainland, was not, however, from a competitive superpower or geopolitical enemy. Thus it should be said that two
things have attended the end of one millennium and the beginning of the other. The first is the introduction of a
reasonably sophisticated philosophical reading of history. This
was Fukuyama's work on how history had come to its natural

fulfilment with the triumph of liberalism and the West. Not only had the West won, it had been destined to win; it was a victory within philosophy as well as history; it was both just, since liberalism and democracy are just, and it was justified by intellectual tools to do with historical progress and philosophical interpretation. In the courts of Washington it is impossible to underestimate the power of such validations. The second is to do with the nagging but, until 9/11, background possibility of challenge from other 'civilizations', principally those associated with Islam. This was the ghost at the feast, and it was Samuel Huntington who most famously writ large the possibility of the ghost gaining flesh. What was just and justified in the US, and the US victory in the Cold War, was threatened by others who were not as just or justified.

8. Until 9/11 the US had no strategy to deal with a 'civilizational' challenge. It probably still doesn't, since the challenge – insofar as it exists in clandestine organizations such as Al Qaeda – does not emanate from countries or geopolitical entities. The military and political need for a visible campaign against terror – with victories – has meant, however, wars on countries. The justification for a war on 'civilizational' challenge, however, has been drawn from a discourse surrounding 9/11, writ large. This large writing concerns certainly a notion of evil (everything that is strange, other-civilizational and rhetorically critical of the US), but it also contains an essential notion of good. The US, in waging war on evil, is doing good in the world. Out of evil will come a legacy of good, but only if the US first defeats evil and delivers the good. Here Fukuyama's philosophical gloss on what was always destined to be called good, and Huntington's warning of the anti-values of other 'civilizations' – making them candidates to be labelled evil – have been added to a US discourse that has developed a sense of righteousness for itself since the founding of the nation.

9. To what are strategic and value-laden considerations might be added a certain underlay of pettiness. There was unfinished business in Iraq from the first Gulf War; there is, but not on

such a large scale, unfinished business in Iran from the days of the US embassy hostages and their protracted ordeal; there is, on the largest scale of all, unfinished business in North Korea, for, whichever side claims victory from the 1950–53 war, both sides know that the war was fought to a bitter standstill, and if an enemy was not defeated it at least was incapable of gaining a victory. Here the temptation to use unrivalled technology, to bomb before the North Koreans have the bomb, to deliver the final and exemplary 'shock and awe', to avoid the casualty-strewn slugfest through the Korean mountains, and to say it is all against manifest evil, might excite the hawks at night as their unrivalled fantasy. How such a defeated and devastated North Korea would be reconstructed is not yet even a dreamwork.

10. If not only against evil, but on behalf of good, what should we reflect upon in this essay? I have tried to give some indications of rich cultures and histories of countries associated with the Axis of Evil. If evil at all, it is not as if evil springs pure and clear out of nothing. It is not a 'found' quality but, at the very least, a profound one that would benefit from an effort at understanding. What, however, about the nature of 'good'? Why is only the West, principally the US, *good* enough to have, perhaps to use, the bomb? Why are others not good enough to develop the bomb? What is the good that hopes to grow out of the evil in which the world seems to find itself in the new millennium, so shortly after 9/11?

Paradisical power

The latest *book-célèbre* in Washington is, by US literary salon standards, brief. Robert Kagan's large-type, 103-small-paged essay appeared in 2003,[3] and might almost have been designed as a riposte to Dominique de Villepin's UN Security Council speech against war in Iraq, representing as it did so much European caution and sensibility. Kagan's book has its own philosophical rubric: not Hegel and Nietzsche as in Fukuyama's writing, but Kant and Hobbes. On the very first page a dichotomy is expressed (but never, thereafter, properly proved) that Europe is turning away from power and entering a self-contained world of laws and rules, transnational cooperation and negotiation –

Kant's world of 'perpetual peace' – whereas the US continues to embrace power, since it understands that the world is anarchic, a place where laws are unreliable, a place that is still in a Hobbesian state, 'red in tooth and claw'.

Kagan's use of these two philosophers is of course gratuitous, and designed simply to illustrate the dichotomy he perceives between the US and Europe. It is an odd and lazy choice all the same. There could not have been a US founded on 'self-evident' rights and constitutional values without the sort of thinking associated with Kant. The idea of a *recht*, law that mirrored a natural and universal justice, was for Kant a 'categorical imperative'. You could not have law that was not, in this larger sense, just. This large universal justice established the preconditions for all things moral. You could not demonstrate empirically that this natural and universal justice existed any more than you could demonstrate an empirical Spirit of History. The idea of motivating spirit, however, whether of history or of justice, was a huge and pervasive idea from the Western Enlightenment,[4] and the founding fathers of the US said it was 'self-evident' because their own sense and spirit of liberty chimed with their sense that there was a greater spirit of liberty that infused the universe. Theirs was a struggle *against* power, and the entire idea of the Constitution and Bill of Rights was to establish laws and rules. The US Declaration of Independence was anti-British, but it was very European.

By contrast, Hobbes was not really writing about power at all. He was writing about security – how a social contract is established on the basis of all subjects seeking a guarantee of their security in a sovereign ruler. Hobbes himself was much beset by political and religious enemies in his lifetime, and had to flee to France for his own safety. The sovereign ruler does indeed have power, but only on the basis that he does deliver sustained security. All the Enlightenment writers, in a long line after Hobbes, sought to establish limits – both philosophical and constitutional – on the powers of the sovereign, while seeking to maintain a guarantee of security, and seeking to guarantee also those Kantian rights that were so 'self-evident' in the US and increasingly large parts of Europe. Even Hobbes sought to establish modest but real limits on the powers of the sovereign. He did not provide a free licence for power, and still more nor did his successors, whereas there could not be a constitution in the US or any part of post-Napoleonic Europe without Kant. When Kagan draws a distinction between Hobbesian US and Kantian Europe, this is philosophically ridiculous. Having said that, his essay does go on to make some pertinent but disturbing points about the international relations of today.

There is a sense, however, throughout this book that what Kagan is doing is seeking to come to grips with a post-Cold War world in which, irritatingly, the West was the victor – not just the US. In short, there arose after 1989 a unipolar world, but it was established on a bipolar alliance. Get rid of this bipolarity, i.e. reduce the influence of Europe, in Kagan's view by lecturing the Europeans on their essential powerlessness, and the US and its vocation of power can be set free from a cultured but irritating anchor.

In this view of the world the attitude of the British prime minister is entirely if narrowly sensible: persuade Europe that the US is the only game in town and be an influence within an intimate alliance with the US on foreign policy or, failing that, insert Britain – come British hell or high water – into such an intimate alliance that the US president must consult the British on the future of the world. There may be something wise about this, or there may be something Faustian. In the meantime the battalions of British sceptics might suggest that Britain, despite itself, is more European than it thinks. Having said that, this prime minister is in a long line of British prime ministers since Churchill who have prioritized relationships with the US over those with Europe. Margaret Thatcher's 'special relationship' with Ronald Reagan set a standard that others would follow – not only of allied states, but of personal camaraderie and the intimation of intimate friendship. John Major had a less obviously intimate relationship with the first George Bush but still allied Britain to the US in the first Gulf War – but then so did France, most of Europe, most of the Islamic states and even Syria. The thing about the second Gulf War is the aloneness of the US president and British prime minister. The Spaniards and

Italians did not fight. The Australian force was minuscule. The two meaningful Western belligerents both chose intimacy and had intimacy thrust upon them by virtue of mass desertion. In this sense of course Robert Kagan is right to pick up on a rift between the US and Europe, although it was properly a rift between the US and most of the world.

The thing is, however, the observation of senior and significant US power is not new. It has been made by commentators and academics for years, even at the height of efforts towards multilateral agreements or 'regimes' of behaviour over, for example, trade, 'regimes' that were meant to bind states as much as having been devised by them in concert. The regime or concert was seen by some as having become, or being on the verge of becoming, more powerful than the states themselves, including even the US. This was over-optimistic. Specialists in regime theory and analysis such as Robert Keohane made the pertinent point that the most successful complex regimes required a single hegemon, around which other participants would cluster.[5] The British international specialist Susan Strange on more than one occasion lamented the 'myth' that the US was in danger of losing its hegemony.[6] The US is, both in these analyses and in observable post-Cold War history, the most powerful state in the world. Kagan has no need to labour that fact. What is irritating about his book is his advice that Europe should accept and love and cooperate with US power, and particularly the grounds on which he offers this advice.

The first on which I wish to comment is the historical line he draws between his contention that the US - by coming to the assistance of Europe during and after the Second World War - effectively helped create modern Europe, and that today's Europe, after benefiting from and building upon that provisioned start, has entered a 'postmodern paradise' where the struggle that modernity entailed no longer commands centre-stage respect. Instead Europe celebrates a consciousness of itself that is centred upon its own possible integration, and this emphasizes the fact that 'compromise and reconciliation is possible after generations of prejudice, war and suffering'.[7] For Kagan this is worrying because Europe now insists upon the possibility of compromise and reconciliation internationally. This is the nub of divergence between the US and Europe: one has power which it feels it should exercise to eradicate threats to international peace; the other wishes to incorporate, by persuasion and reason, even its antagonists into Kantian 'perpetual peace'.

My difficulty with this is that Kagan's account is both an exaggeration and a caricature. The US was of significant, pivotal, even decisive help during and after the Second World War, but this was not solely because it wished to help Europe. There were strategic interests at heart that were very firmly lodged within the US, not least with those concerned with the non-European theatre of the Pacific and Asia, and those to do with the post-Nazi rise of Communism. Not only that, it was involvement in the Second World War that facilitated the US post-war position as the first superpower. The atom bomb was developed because of the exigencies of war. In that sense the military rush to modernity created the US as much as the US might claim to have created the modern Europe.

Kagan's account is a caricature when it comes to Europe's role simply as a purveyor of compromise and reconciliation. That did not seem to be the case in Margaret Thatcher's Falklands adventure, in various Belgian and French adventures in Africa, and Britain's own intervention in Sierra Leone. Europe was indeed indecisive about what to do in the Balkans, but it is now the war crimes tribunal in The Hague that is trying those who committed atrocities, and that is an institutional precedent against which the US fights shy. All power and no answerability is itself an irresponsibility.

The second of Kagan's arguments with which I have difficulty is his approval of Robert Cooper's idea of necessary double standards. Within Europe, law and cooperative security are fine. Outside Europe, however, 'we need to revert to the rougher methods of an earlier era – force, preemptive attack, deception, whatever is necessary … among ourselves we keep the law, but when we are operating in the jungle we must also use the laws of the jungle.'[8] The point is that the Europeans, above all, are masters of double standards. It is not just Albion that is perfidious. All of Italy is a stylish balancing act between formal and informal modes of operation, i.e. operations within and despite the law. Kagan's complaint is that today, here and now, especially over Iraq, most of Europe did not want to fight with the US. However, in the first Gulf War, it did. Kagan's rush to judgement is itself postmodern in that it ignores the very recent past and privileges a fragment of the immediate past. It is not that there are for Europe no double standards; it is that there are preconditions for adopting any standard. These might be indeed to do with law, but might also be to do with just cause, or justified cause at least. If not justice, many European states are infamously alert to the black arts of justification. 'Spin' in Britain is a prominent example. Law and highly subtle double standards are a blend that Kagan might have missed, although, having said that, the very possibility in Britain of a Hutton Inquiry, the thoroughness with which it was conducted - including the vast amount of otherwise secret material that was subpoenaed - even despite its outcome and consequences, are testimony that in a real and basic sense law within Europe, at least within the UK, is alive, and that declared standards have preconditions of good behaviour.

Finally, Kagan insists that power, force, Hobbesian rule of the jungle are today necessary because 'surely militant Muslim fundamentalism is an implacable enemy of the West'.[9] This statement prompts many questions. In what way 'surely'? If 'surely', why? What does 'militant Muslim fundamentalism' mean? (And is not the distinction between power as a necessary right and law as a European parochialism a little fundamentalist in its cleavage?) And if indeed there is a 'Muslim fundamentalist' challenge, how exactly is force to be used against it? Has flattening Iraq, which was a secular state, done anything to erase or diminish the 'fundamentalist' threat? It has done nothing of the sort. Kagan's enemy is far too generalized, its threat described as an unspecified foreboding, its rationale not understood, understanding replaced only by force.

Kagan concludes his little book by saying that there is no need for a 'clash of civilizations' within the West[10] - between the civilization of law and the civilization of power, provided of course that law becomes a disciple of power. This seems to be

Rome lecturing Greece, forgetting that Greece conquered a very great deal of the world before the Roman era, and forgetting also that Rome could never subdue Persia. If it had not received so much attention in the US it would be tempting to dismiss Kagan's book as silly.

The good that men do

One of the key assumptions of Kagan's book is that the US is *right* to use its power. The more widespread claim made on behalf of the US is that its power is a force for *good*, but this is a problematic claim. If we start with Kagan then, yes, it claims to do good; however, because it necessarily practises double standards, is prepared to be ruthless and is prepared to be unlawful, it is also a force for bad. There will be 'collateral damage' from being good in this manner. The claim might seek to redeem itself by saying, yes, this is true but, despite this, the US accomplishes *more* good than bad. This would be an unfortunate statement because it instantly turns a debate on good into a debate on relativities: how much good outweighs how much bad? Moreover it opens up the debate to a laundry list of things that are discerned to be bad. Some would say that the US stance on environmental pollution and greenhouse emissions is internationally bad. Others would say that the liberal licence given to US pharmaceutical companies to charge high prices is internationally bad. To coin an appropriately unlovely term, it can only result in the diseasification of the world. And this is even before critics would come to issues of political foreign policy. The claim that, despite this, good is accomplished would have its own checklist. The US, although not in per capita terms, disburses a huge aid budget. Much of it is, however, politically tied (Israel is by far the largest recipient) or finances US expertise abroad or dumps food that simultaneously feeds hungry nations but makes their farmers redundant or uncompetitive.[11]

More fundamentally (perhaps, according to critics, in its own way more fundamentalistically), the claim is that the US promotes international liberalism, democracy, accountability and transparency. International economic liberalism, however, benefits US trading practices above most others; the installation of democracy in Iraq was premised on a shoot-first, consult-later strategy which is not at all certain of creating a democracy that will have no organic roots or authenticity. As for accountability, Kagan's entire account of power is that the US at least is not accountable to Europe, or anyone else, and, as the aftermath of inquiries and postmortems carries on in both the US and Britain, the going to war with Iraq in the first place is increasingly seen as not having been entirely transparent. There are genuine benefits of US policy abroad, but these are alongside many difficulties. Finally, it is to do with the measure of relativities and this makes the question of good a problematic one. It is even more problematic if this good is proposed as the alternative to evil – if this is the good that is to deliver the world out of evil.

Let us look thoughtfully at this delivery by good out of evil. Surmounting the discussion in the last paragraph is the basic observation that 9/11 demonstrated that there are many people in the world who think that the US does more bad than good. It would be wilful ignorance to give this no weight. The US response was to go out and attack evil, but without properly asking why evil had attacked the US. The formulation discussed above may be summarized as follows: war against evil is not limited war for a limited objective, so, in accordance with the traditional norms of just war, this war is not just; since this war is part of a grand and sweeping strategy, whether of full-spectrum dominance, drawing forward lines in the civilizational sand, or against groups vaguely described as Muslim fundamentalists, it is *justified* as being moral; it is moral because it is against evil; those who fight evil are *ipso facto* good; their use of power is, by extension, also good.

There are various leaps in this formulation – which all the same distils the discourse of the US hawks – but the main problem is that following on from this formulation is the view that, therefore, power justifies the good. I have tried to be precise in that last sentence. It is not that good justifies the use of power, although that is there as a rhetorical sub-clause. It is, in terms of Kagan's essay, power that justifies the good because it is only power that allows the vocation of good to be exercised. European negotiation and reconciliation cannot. Good that is not spread abroad as an international vocation is itself powerless. It is power

..... gives life to good, it is power that allows a moral choice not only to be posed but to be made. Without power, internationally there is no good. That which is morally good, i.e. that which is against evil, depends on power. It is not power that depends on good. Power justifies the notion of good as an active principle. Otherwise it is only an abstract one.

Now this is problematic because of an active difficulty. At what stage does power become a moral quality in its own right? Kagan's book comes close to making it so. Donald Rumsfeld's speeches have made it so. Is it therefore a twenty-first-century world of power and evil? And that the delivery out of evil will leave us principally with the US as the incarnation of power? Perhaps that was, and will be, the reason why people and groups attack the US.

Of course, this is to render the world and discourse of the Washington hawks into a single dimension. Moreover, whatever 'heartland America' is, it is still a place where notions of good and of morality play a major role. What I am trying to address here is the difficulty that is created when both hawks and heartland speak in two dimensions: either power and evil, or good and evil. Whichever term is chosen, good or power, or whether the two are conflated - as in the president's speeches - either or both are in opposition to evil. There is a sharp divide between two moral qualities here that is Manichean.

Near the beginning of this essay I gave a summarized account of Manicheanism: it had implicitly or explicitly within its teachings the idea that there were two Creators, one of good and one of evil. What the orthodox church has done, over the many years of Manichean challenge, has been to develop and refine early Judaic images of the devil, or Satan. If there are two spiritual principles within the universe, one of them is not a God equal to the other, but fallen - though he had indeed sought to depose God by waging war against him - and, because fallen, damned.

Here there are two basic propositions. The first is the Manichean one proper: that good and evil are two opposed spiritual and moral principles. The second is the orthodox Christian refinement: although good and evil are two opposed principles, the principle of good is stronger, and that of evil is a fallen principle. Evil has already lost to good, but on earth is making a futile last stand before entering damnation.

There are two applications of Manicheanism in the contemporary War on Evil. The first is that the sense and imagery of fundamentally opposed principles looms large over the rhetoric and discourse of President Bush and his coterie of hawks.[12] The second is that, as also noted earlier in this essay, it informed the discourse also of the clerical party after the Iranian revolution. Today, eccentrically but unmistakably, it infuses the North Korean reply to US accusations about its nuclear armament aspirations and programme.

There are two further observations to make about all this. The first is to note the core of the North Korean complaint about US pressure. Shorn of its eccentricity, and disregarding for a moment the nature of the Kim Jong Il regime, there is the pungent observation that the US thinks only it, and its most trusted allies, or others approved by it, are *good* enough to have the bomb. Given my disquisition on the relationship between US good and US power, it is a clear proposition that the ambition is to curtail not only North Korean power, but any sense of North Korean good. Put more colloquially, it avoids the effort required to take the difficult quasi-mystical Stalinism of Kim Il Sung and Kim Jong Il seriously. The second observation is very simple, and begins with the question: why not take not only the North Koreans but all 'fundamentalist' Muslim and other evil enemies of the US seriously? If this does not happen there is a different formulation of Manicheanism that is possible: that the early twenty-first century is seeing the shaping of a war between a fundamental statement of US power and what the US calls fundamentalism. If two self-enclosed bodies of thought and value, each accusing the other of being the more self-enclosed, are going to slug it out, then there will not be much room for negotiation (however 'European' that is), or even thoughtful discussion. As Susan Sontag has said in her latest essay: 'There's nothing wrong with standing back and thinking. To paraphrase several sages: "Nobody can think and hit someone at the same time."'[13]

Of course it is much more difficult to do this than to say it. To make a nuclear bomb requires a universally agreed form and

)lication of physics. To deploy that bomb within a strategic doctrine is meant to require an agreed formulation of rational choice theory and games theory. It may contain grotesqueries, such as Herman Kahn's 'ladder of escalation', but the formulation of rational choice is meant to be agreed.[14] All that might throw this is a different form of rationality. Without investigating the possibility of such different forms, the world will be unsafe, not because more states will acquire the bomb but because we won't quite know what they will do with it. The choice is either to make those investigations or to insist upon the hegemony of one sort of rationality shared by one small club of those with the bomb. The first is a choice that opens itself to pluralism, the second is a fundamental choice.

Someone who has heroically sought to make the first choice is the Catholic theologian Hans Kung. Together with Helmut Schmidt – the former German chancellor and early formulator of swift, flexible but rational nuclear doctrine – he convened a Parliament of the World's Religions and an Inter-Action Council, both designed to debate and produce agreed declarations on global ethics and global responsibilities.[15] The declarations, when finally agreed, were superb manifestations of human spirit and spiritual value. The road to agreement was terrible: the Islamic delegation wanted the declaration of the Parliament of the World's Religions prefaced with the traditional Koranic phrase 'In the name of God', but the Buddhist delegation objected on the grounds that in Buddhism there is no God. But Kung did it, and demonstrated that pluralism can, even with difficulty, agree on common standards and common ethics. His was neither a Manichean nor a one-rationality-fits-all project. One of the problems of international relations as applied science is that its underlying academic discipline is also deeply wedded to a single source of rationality: it is either Western science that both builds the bomb and then predicts its use, or Western philosophy that debates whether history has ended or whether power or negotiation are better. Hegel, Nietzsche, Hobbes and Kant form a terrifyingly narrow representation of thought upon which to couch pronouncements on the end of certain worlds and the beginnings of new worlds. Something more pluralistic needs to break out or break over what becomes in itself an invitation to only a sophisticated Manicheanism: Western Enlightenment thought (perhaps with its postmodern critique), and all other thought 'out there', beyond the US and beyond even Europe.[16] We might never agree, as Kung's councils never agreed, on what might be 'true', but we might agree upon what is actually good. We might also begin to understand what we have called 'evil'. Perhaps if this is what comes out of evil, this might be a good thing.

6

IN PRAISE OF CHEESE-EATING SURRENDER MONKEYS *OR* WASHINGTON FUNDAMENTALISTS VS PARISIAN MONKEYS

The Chinese Year of the Monkey is under way at the time of writing. I want to end this essay with a reference to how I began it. The US was unprepared for 9/11. Its response was to vent its fury outwards but, in so doing, it probably did little to overcome the causes of 9/11 or to prevent episodes of terrorism against the US from happening again. In fact its response probably invited future terrorism. At the beginning of this essay I cited the bipartisan report, *New World Coming*, which forewarned in 1999 that the US would 'be attacked by terrorists using weapons of mass destruction, and Americans will lose their lives on American soil, possibly in large numbers.' This of course happened in 2001. In July 2003 another bipartisan group, this time a Senate and House joint inquiry into the causes of 9/11, released a 900-page report.[1] It makes pretty damning reading, not of evil or terrorist groups – these have by now become a given – but of US preparedness and the operational methods and political oversight of US intelligence.

The report is critical not of the lack of intelligence – there was plenty of that available – but of the fragmented nature of it and of the lack of political will among the various intelligence agencies to piece it all together. Moreover, and this is surprising in a land of technological leadership, many FBI offices and officers had no internet access and agents wrote their reports in longhand and in triplicate. Information was hoarded: the FBI withheld information from the CIA and vice versa. Such intelligence warnings as did get through, such as reports of Middle

Eastern men taking flying lessons without any particular interest in learning how to land, were ignored. There was, in short, not only a lack of coordination but a lack of overarching doctrine when it came to the idea of foreign terrorism within the US. The idea was abstract, and nobody joined up the myriad dots of intelligence that would have drawn a concrete picture of danger.

Of course, since 9/11 a very great deal has been done to prevent these lapses re-occurring. The efforts have stopped short, however, of reforming a fundamental distortion in intelligence expenditure. In the US the CIA administers only between 15 and 20 per cent of the annual foreign intelligence budget. The Pentagon administers almost all the rest. It is the Pentagon that directs the mission of spy satellites and eavesdropping ships and, as noted at the beginning of this essay, the Pentagon has no military doctrine of how to engage an enemy that is not contained within conventional geopolitical space. It does not know how to gather the sort of intelligence it needs to fight the kind of war it cannot fight. Add to this the report's criticism of the very small numbers of Arabic speakers within the intelligence community (there were almost no Pashtun-speaking agents when the war with Afghanistan was launched), and the picture looks as parlous as the CIA's budget for a task which the Pentagon also wants to do, but does not know how.

There are two additional and hugely significant political problems highlighted by the report. The first is the problem of Saudi Arabia. It is clear that significant funds reached Osama Bin Laden and Al Qaeda from sources within Saudi Arabia. Some of these could even be clearly identified and named. Yet this is a taboo topic. The White House forced the bipartisan inquiry to delete 28 pages of testimony about Saudi financial support for terrorist groups. The second political problem is that the CIA will never secure any of the intelligence funding now devoted to the Pentagon because neither Donald Rumsfeld nor any other defense secretary will sacrifice power and resources. The US had itself partly to blame for not preventing 9/11, and will have itself partly to blame again should another major terrorist attack succeed – even if Syria, Iran and North Korea have by that time been invaded, conquered and subjugated. The problem with

Washington is that it is reluctant to change. Even if cyclically, it
will seek to change the world into its own image, but it will not
change itself. It is not a place for the timorous, for surrender
monkeys, and even the second George Bush would not pick a
fight with Rumsfeld and his hawks. The marginalization of Colin
Powell is a warning to all. Even with a fresh administration the
world is unlikely to become a more reconciled, 'European' place.

But, cutting now to Europe, to Paris in particular, there could
not be more of a contrast with Washington and its huge monu-
ments to itself and its own history – right or wrong, but
unchanging. Clustered near the Champs Elysées there are broad
avenues named after Presidents John F. Kennedy, Franklin
Roosevelt and Woodrow Wilson. There is an avenue named after
New York and an Avenue Rockefeller running through the
university residences district. Franklin Roosevelt also has a metro
station bearing his name. No other nation, apart from France
itself, is so honoured (the avenue named after Winston Churchill is rather small). There is a plaque to commemorate where
Ernest Hemingway lived, and the epitome of a French man of
letters who was also a fighting man of action, André Malraux,
dedicated his (in)famous memoirs to 'Mrs John Fitzgerald Kennedy'. There was a recent time when France, above all, believed
the myth of Camelot and, even in the US, France seemed the
home of philosophy, art, style and romance. If times have
changed, Paris has bestowed its affections on others, not by
names but by appreciation of cultures. Looking down the broad
avenues in two directions from the Arc de Triomphe, one sees at
one end the brutal modernism of the new Defence Arch. It
contrasts deliberately with the baroque and fussy quality of the
Arc de Triomphe. This much is France talking to France. But, at
the other end, nestled in the courtyard of the Louvre, is the
amazing glass pyramid of the Chinese-American architect George
Pei. The pyramid is amazing in itself, and the French arms of the
Louvre seem to cradle it. What is more amazing is how the
transparent structure lets the visitor go down into an under-
ground antechamber, from which the histories of the many
cultures on earth can be accessed. When the Arc de Triomphe

looks in this direction, it is France talking to a multicultural history that has not yet ended.

Of course this is a romantic depiction. The barbarities, conceits and perfidies of France are as great and ugly as those of any power. Its colonial empire wreaked as much havoc upon the lives of others as the British Empire did, and as the nascent new form of US Empire already does. More innocent people have paid with their lives in Afghanistan and Iraq than died in New York on 9/11. What the French, however, have learnt from their own conceits and deceits is a kind of worldliness. Theirs is not a particularly naive political community. Self-aware turpitude is not too strong an at least occasional description. Even so, Dominique de Villepin's rejection of war in Iraq, in his speech to the UN Security Council, was the height of what worldliness is capable of when it perceives something, not just as being more wrong than right, but as being simply wrong. The operative words here are 'wrong', and 'simply'. The US view of the world which seems to threaten it is simple. I have tried in this essay not to justify or excuse various states that are members or candidates for membership of the US Axis of Evil, but to render them slightly more complex than they might seem to a president who had left his continent only once and who had visited a total of three countries before attaining the most powerful office in the world. His advisers may have had more sophisticated histories, but I have tried to argue that their hawkish doctrine is also - despite recourse to Kant and Hobbes - simple. Power and dominance should not be simple things. Power to do what? Dominance over what? The 'what' should not be an unknown quantity. It should have, in fact, its own quality, and this should be known to policy makers. Cultures and histories, after all, are not things to be shifted around a chessboard, or given notional or no values in a game of rational choice. Simply having the power to destroy does not, by itself, give anyone or any state a prerogative to rule the world - to have full-spectrum dominance. André Malraux, in that part of his memoirs titled 'The Temptation of the West', quoted from the Indian *Rig Veda*. This is Vishnu speaking:

I am Death
I am Death that snatches all ...

and I am beautiful speech, memory, steadfastness and forgiveness.

With the power of death should come other highly responsible qualities. When Robert Jungk wrote his book on how the atomic bomb was developed,[2] he borrowed its title, *Brighter than 1000 Suns*, from the *Bhagavad-Gita*: 'If the radiance of a thousand suns were to burst into the sky, that would be like the splendour of the Mighty One.' The Mighty One could create and sustain many very different things, as well as destroy. Malraux acquired some of his Indian knowledge at the Benares Hindu University, among 'sacred trees, rooms in English Gothic style, professors in yellow robes'.[3] That seems an almost ideal mixture for the dawn of the twenty-first century.

I am not sure what Malraux meant by calling part of his memoirs 'The Temptation of the West'. It is a mixture of philosophical adventures in India and near-death experiences in wartime France. He seems to have been a tank commander, charging the German lines, with a Chinese gunner. I think Malraux was trying to say that the West was dying of its own weight in having tried to do too much. It was about to be recycled back into Vishnu's great ebb and flow of time, creation, death and re-creation. But there is a particularly beautiful and poignant, momentary description. It is a rare intersection between Indian mysticism and the French war against the Germans. The tank has crashed. Malraux and his crew are lucky to be alive. On the French battlefield he remembers a passage from the *Bhagavad-Gita*. The great battle between the Pandava brothers and their enemies is over. The opposing king lies pinioned by arrows. 'Beneath the moon which had lit up our tank like a funeral lamp, the Chinese face of Prade with its three teeth had answered nothing – beneath that gleam which had guided the monkeys round the body of the old blind king on the battlefield of the *Bhagavad-Gita*.'[4] Sometimes it is those called monkeys who watch over the fitful ends and starts of history.

NOTES

Preface

[1] For an excellent history of European and American reactions (and revulsions) to the Chinese, see Jonathan D. Spence, *The Chan's Great Continent: China in Western Minds* (New York: W.W. Norton, 1998). See also L.H.M. Ling, *Conquest Desire: Postcolonial Learning between Asia and the West* (New York: St Martin's Press, 2001).

[2] One of the great first tests of brinksmanship at least, fortified albeit hopefully by calculations of choice and which path the Soviets would *rationally* choose (in a largely irrational political situation), was the 1962 Cuban missile crisis. The memoir by President Kennedy's brother still conveys some of the delicate hopes that hung around what was meant to be a rational drive to the brink. See Robert F. Kennedy, *13 Days* (London: Macmillan, 1969).

Chapter 1. From Cold War Towards a New Clash?

[1] For the various volumes of the Commission's reports, see www.cfr.org and www.nssg.gov. One of the Commission's members and co-chair, the former US senator and presidential candidate, Gary Hart, has spoken and written widely about the Commission's findings and this particular conclusion. I found a truncated version of one of his articles as far afield as Zimbabwe: 'US Seeks "Grand Strategy" to Fight Terror', *Daily News* (Harare), 16 July 2003.

[2] Samuel P. Huntington, *The Clash of Civilizations and the Remaking of World Order* (New York: Simon & Schuster, 1996). This was the stretched version of his short article, 'The Clash of Civilizations?', *Foreign Affairs*, 72 (Summer 1993).

[3] There is much rich work on Gnosticism. By far the best remains that by Elaine Pagels, *The Gnostic Gospels* (New York: Random House, 1979).

[4] Again, for an elegant history, see Elaine Pagels, *The Origin of Satan* (London: Allen Lane, 1996).

[5] Ralph K. White, *Nobody Wanted War* (New York: Doubleday, 1968).

[6] See Simon Dalby, *Creating the Second Cold War: The Discourse of Politics* (London: Pinter, 1990).

7   Bernard Brodie, *War and Politics* (New York: Macmillan, 1973), Chapter 7.

8   Quoted in William W. Kaufmann, *Military Policy and National Security* (Princeton: Princeton University Press, 1972), pp 13-15.

9   *Ibid.*, p 136.

10 Throughout the Cold War, British thinking on the strategic deployment and control of nuclear weapons was marked by combinations of pragmatism, rationality and the sense of the special vulnerability of Europe. See inter alia, A.J.R. Groom, *British Thinking about Nuclear Weapons* (London: Pinter, 1974); Robert O'Neill and David N. Schwartz (eds), *Hedley Bull on Arms Control* (London: Macmillan, 1987); Laurence Martin, *The Two-Edged Sword* (London: Weidenfeld & Nicolson, 1982); and Mark Hoffman (ed), *UK Arms Control in the 1990s* (Manchester: Manchester University Press, 1990).

11 Herman Kahn, *On Escalation: Metaphors and Scenarios* (London: Pall Mall, 1965). See also Herman Kahn's two other major works, *On Thermonuclear War* (Princeton: Princeton University Press, 1961) and *Thinking about the Unthinkable* (London: Weidenfeld & Nicolson, 1962).

12 Anatol Rapoport, 'Introduction' to Karl Von Clausewitz, *On War* (London: Pelican, 1968).

13 See Klaus Knorr and James N. Rosenau (eds), *Contending Approaches to International Politics* (Princeton: Princeton University Press, 1969).

14 It should be added that the Chinese had their own reasons for hosting Kissinger and Nixon, and most Chinese political historians – for very good reasons – would prioritize the role of Zhou Enlai over that of Kissinger. See Kuo-kang Shao, *Zhou Enlai and the Foundations of Chinese Foreign Policy* (London: Macmillan, 1996), pp 199-209.

15 Michael Nicholson, *Rationality and the Analysis of International Conflict* (Cambridge: Cambridge University Press, 1992).

16 For a brilliant example of how this can be done, though in the field of development economics, not international relations, see Partha Dasgupta, *An Inquiry into Well-Being and Destitution* (Oxford: Oxford University Press, 1993).

17 Martin Hollis and Steve Smith, *Explaining and Understanding in International Relations* (Oxford: Clarendon, 1991), pp 181-3.

18 E.P. Thompson, Mary Kaldor, et al, *Mad Dogs: The US Raids on Libya* (London: Pluto, 1986).

19 John Davis, *Libyan Politics: Tribe and Revolution* (London: I.B. Tauris, 1987).

[20] Although this is certainly not how the Third World actors saw or sought to see themselves. For an analysis of how Southern African states tried to construct independent foreign policies, see Stephen Chan, *Exporting Apartheid: Foreign Policies in Southern Africa 1978–1988* (London: Macmillan, 1990).

[21] The term and idea of a Second Cold War is most closely associated with Fred Halliday. See his *The Making of the Second Cold War* (London: Verso, 1983) and his *Cold War, Third World: An Essay on Soviet–American Relations* (London: Hutchinson Radius, 1989). In this latter work, Halliday tends to see the 1986 US bombing of Libya as part of the bipolar game (p 36), but I see it very much as a one-off. Libya could not be said to be within the Soviet view of the main game. It was a domestic point-scoring exercise for President Reagan and, if it was part of his foreign policy – what came to be called the 'Reagan doctrine' of intervention and interventionist rhetoric – it was a cheap hit, not a key target.

[22] Michel Foucault, *Politics, Philosophy, Culture: Interviews and Other Writings 1977–1984* (ed Lawrence D. Kritzman) (New York: Routledge, 1988), p 213.

[23] Annabelle Sreberny-Mohammadi and Ali Mohammadi, *Small Media, Big Revolution: Communication, Culture, and the Iranian Revolution* (Minneapolis: University of Minnesota Press, 1994), pp 165, 167.

[24] Nikki R. Keddie, 'Iranian Revolutions in Comparative Perspective', in Albert Hourani, Philip S. Khoury and Mary C. Wilson (eds), *The Modern Middle East: A Reader* (Berkeley: University of California Press, 1993), p 617.

[25] Asghar Schirazi, *The Constitution of Iran: Politics and the State in the Islamic Republic* (London: I.B. Tauris, 1998).

[26] Mahmoud Sariolghalam, 'The Determinants of Iraqi Foreign Policy Behaviour in the 1980s', in Stephen Chan and Andrew J. Williams (eds), *Renegade States: The Evolution of Revolutionary Foreign Policy* (Manchester: Manchester University Press, 1994), p 191.

[27] James Piscatori (ed), *Islamic Fundamentalisms and the Gulf Crisis* (Chicago: American Academy of Arts and Sciences, 1991).

[28] Paul Kennedy, *The Rise and Fall of the Great Powers* (London: Unwin Hyman, 1988).

[29] Actual Japanese reception of this work was mixed. For a riposte, see E. Usuki, 'An End to the "End of History" Debates', *International Relations* (Japanese-language journal), 99 (1992).

[30] For Fukuyama's debt to his teacher, Alexandre Kojeve, and Kojeve's interpretation of Hegel, see Paul Bacon, 'The End of History and the First Man of the Twenty-First Century', in Stephen Chan and

Jarrod Wiener (eds), *Twentieth-Century International History* (London: I.B. Tauris, 1999).

31 Francis Fukuyama, 'The End of History?', *The National Interest*, 16 (Summer 1989).

32 Francis Fukuyama, *The End of History and the Last Man* (London: Penguin, 1992).

33 For an early and prescient series of reflections on the future, see Chris Brown (ed), *Political Restructuring in Europe: Ethical Perspectives* (London: Routledge, 1994).

34 The only English edition I could find was published in Croatia: Alain Finkielkraut, *The Crime of Being Born* (Zagreb: Ceres, 1997). The last appendix, a chronology of the Balkan war of the 1990s by Jadranka Brncic, is especially helpful. I should add that chronologies of this war have proved particularly contentious. Who records which events and why? For a discussion of this, see David Campbell, *National Deconstruction: Violence, Identity and Justice in Bosnia* (Minneapolis: University of Minnesota Press, 1998).

35 For a good history, see Sabrina P. Ramet, *Nationalism and Federalism in Yugoslavia 1962–1991* (Bloomington: Indiana University Press, 1992). If some observant readers are confused as to whether this book and a 1984 book of the same title, the latter authored by Pedro Ramet, are the same book - yes, they are first and second editions of the same work. In between, the author changed sex and, hence, name. There is now a third edition, to which I have not had access, but sex and name have remained constant. See also Christopher Cviic, *Remaking the Balkans* (London: Royal Institute of International Affairs, 1991). I cite these books since much else, written after the tragic events of the 1990s, seems like wise hindsight.

36 For a brief but helpful historical note, see Sir Reginald Hibbert, *The Kosovo Question: Origins, Present Complications and Prospects* (London: David Davies Memorial Institute Occasional Paper 11, May 1999).

37 Joan Peters, *From Time Immemorial: The Origins of the Arab–Jewish Conflict over Palestine* (London: Michael Joseph, 1984). This was a very controversial volume, not least because of its author's ethnicization of the conflict by her choice of group-names in the title.

38 Primo Levi, *If Not Now, When?* (London: Abacus, 1987), pp 190–2.

39 Sydney D. Bailey, *Four Arab–Israeli Wars and the Peace Process* (London: Macmillan, 1990), p 422.

40 Henry Kissinger, *A World Restored: Metternich, Castlereagh and the Problems of Peace 1812–22* (London: Weidenfeld & Nicolson, 1957). This was Kissinger's own Harvard PhD, written in record time, but from whose ideas he never subsequently deviated.

41   Huntington, *The Clash of Civilizations and the Remaking of World Order*, pp 26-7.
42   Thomas Sowell, *Race and Culture: A World View* (New York: Basic Books, 1994).
43   Edward W. Said, 'A Window on the World', *The Guardian* (Review), 2 August 2003. This was an adaptation, more pointed it seems, of the Introduction to the 25th anniversary edition of *Orientalism* (London: Penguin, 2003).
44   Huntington, 'The Clash of Civilizations?'.
45   Edward W. Said, *Reflections on Exile* (London: Granta, 2000), Chapter 46.
46   Akbar S. Ahmed, *Postmodernism and Islam: Predicament and Promise* (London: Routledge, 1992).
47   Kaveh L. Afrasiabi, 'On the "Clash of Civilizations"', *Telos*, 115 (2000).
48   Kaveh L. Afrasiabi, 'The Contest of Civilizations and Interreligious Dialogue', *The Iranian Journal of International Affairs*, XI:3 (1999).
49   And I do admit that I have done precisely this. See my review of Huntington's book and Huntington's reply, accusing me of writing a splenetic review, in Stephen Chan, 'Too Neat and Under-Thought a World Order: Huntington and Civilisations', and Samuel P. Huntington, 'The Clash of Civilizations - A Response', *Millennium*, 26:1 (1997). Unable to avoid spleen's temptation, I repeated my points in Stephen Chan, 'Reliving the Boxer Uprising; or, the Restricted Meaning of Civilisation', in Peter Mandaville and Andrew Williams (eds), *Meaning and International Relations* (London: Routledge, 2003).
50   The US scholar who has done a very great deal of highly original (and imaginative) work on this is James Der Derian, *Antidiplomacy: Spies, Terror, Speed, and War* (Oxford: Blackwell, 1992). For a good recent summary of his research interests in this direction, see James Der Derian, 'Virtual Security: Technical Oversight, Simulated Foresight and Political Blindspots in the Infosphere', in Chan and Wiener (eds), *Twentieth-Century International History*. (May I be excused a debating point with my publishers here: this was the chapter the book's referees wanted taking out because they thought cyberwar had no relationship to real war.)

Chapter 2. The First Man and the Students of God

1   From Brian Stone's translation of *Sir Gawain and the Green Knight* (London: Penguin, 1959), Stanza 38.

2 This term crops up often in Faridu'd-Din Attar's epic philosophical poem, *The Speech of the Birds* (Cambridge: Islamic Texts Society, 1998).

3 Tarif Khalidi (ed), *The Muslim Jesus: Sayings and Stories in Islamic Literature* (Cambridge, MA: Harvard University Press, 2001), p 96.

4 Herbert S. Yee, 'The Three-World Theory and Post-Mao China's Global Strategy', *International Affairs*, 59:2 (1983).

5 I have drawn in this section from my earlier essay: Stephen Chan and Dominic Powell, 'Reform, Insurgency and Counter-Insurgency in Afghanistan', in Paul B. Rich and Richard Stubbs (eds), *The Counter-Insurgent State: Guerilla Warfare and State Building in the Twentieth Century* (London: Macmillan, 1997). For an excellent, detailed account see Raja Anwar, *The Tragedy of Afghanistan: A First-Hand Account* (London: Verso, 1988).

6 Ahmed Rashid, on p 25 of his book, says that notwithstanding the welter of inflated rumours about Omar, this story is probably true. This is the seminal and still by far the best book on the subject. Ahmed Rashid, *Taliban: Islam, Oil and the New Great Game in Central Asia* (London: I.B. Tauris, 2001). Later, updated editions were published by Pan.

7 Quoted in Michael Scott Doran, 'Gods and Monsters', *Guardian*, 8 December 2001. The interpretation of 'Hubal' in the text is Doran's.

8 Davis, *Libyan Politics: Tribe and Revolution*, p 254.

9 From his preface. This quote is from Joan Juliet Buck, 'France's Prophet Provocateur', *Vanity Fair*, January 2003, p 120.

10 Fred Halliday, *Islam and the Myth of Confrontation: Religion and Politics in the Middle East* (London: I.B. Tauris, 1996).

11 Ahmed Rashid, *Taliban.*, p 136.

12 Said, 'A Window on the World', p 6.

13 See, for example, Ali Mohammadi and Muhammad Ahsan, *Globalisation or Recolonisation? The Muslim World in the 21st Century* (London: Ta-Ha, 2002).

14 His principal work was in fact a UN report: Raul Prebisch, *The Economic Development of Latin America and its Principal Problems* (New York: UN, 1950).

15 Well summarized in Magnus Blomstrom and Bjorn Hettne, *Development Theory in Transition: The Dependency Debate and Beyond – Third World Responses* (London: Zed, 1984), pp 172–3.

16 John M. Hobson, *The Wealth of States: A Comparative Sociology of International Economic and Political Change* (Cambridge: Cambridge University Press, 1997).

17 Susan Strange, 'The Westfailure System, 1999', in her collected writings, edited by Roger Tooze and Christopher May, *Authority and Markets: Susan Strange's Writings on International Political Economy* (London: Palgrave Macmillan, 2002), pp 249-50.

18 This is an appendix to Khaled Hroub's *Hamas: Political Thought and Practice* (Washington, DC: Institute for Palestine Studies, 2000), p 274.

19 Wilfred Madelung and Toby Mayer (trans & eds), *Struggling with the Philosopher: Muhammad b. 'Abd al-Karim al-Shahrastani's Kitab al-Musara'a* (London: I.B. Tauris, 2001).

20 Nasir Khusraw (ed & trans Faquir M. Hunzai), *Knowledge and Liberation: A Treatise on Philosophical Theology* (London: I.B. Tauris, 1999).

21 Ali Rahnema, *An Islamic Utopian: A Political Biography of Ali Shari'ati* (London: I.B. Tauris, 2000).

22 Edward W. Said, *Covering Islam* (London: Routledge and Kegan Paul, 1981).

Chapter 3. History's Latest Superpower Goes to War against the First

1 Andrew George's inaugural lecture as Professor of Babylonian at the School of Oriental and African Studies in 2003 traced his ingenious translation of the word for 'toilet'.

2 T.E. Lawrence, *Seven Pillars of Wisdom* (London: Penguin, 1962).

3 For an excellent history, both before but especially after 1958, see Marion Farouk-Sluglett and Peter Sluglett, *Iraq since 1958: From Revolution to Dictatorship* (London: I.B. Tauris, 2001). See also Charles A. Tripp, *A Political History of Iraq* (Cambridge: Cambridge University Press, 2000).

4 Adeed Dawisha, 'Invoking the Spirit of Arabism in the Foreign Policy of Saddam's Iraq', in Adeed Dawisha (ed), *Islam in Foreign Policy* (Cambridge: Cambridge University Press, 1985), p 127.

5 Efraim Karsh and Inari Rautsi, *Saddam Hussein: A Political Biography* (New York: Free Press, 1991), pp 35-6.

6 Mahmoud Sariolghalam, 'The Determinants of Iraqi Foreign Policy Behaviour in the 1980s', in Chan and Williams (eds), *Renegade States*, p 188.

7 James Piscatori, 'Religion and Realpolitik: Islamic Responses to the Gulf War', in Piscatori (ed), *Islamic Fundamentalisms and the Gulf Crisis*, p 3.

8 For good histories of this war, see Dilip Hiro, *The Longest War: The Iran–Iraq Military Conflict* (London: Grafton, 1989); Efraim Karsh (ed), *The Iran–Iraq War: Impact and Implications* (London: Macmillan,

1989); and Shahram Chubin and Charles Tripp, *Iran and Iraq at War* (London: I.B. Tauris, 1988).

9　It is interesting to recall that in 1957 King Faisal of Iraq sought to commission Frank Lloyd Wright to design a new city of Baghdad. The King was assassinated just one year later but Wright's plans apparently still exist. See Karen Glaser's report in the *Guardian*, 18 August 2003.

10　Mahmoud Sariolghalam, 'The Determinants of Iraqi Foreign Policy Behaviour in the 1980s', p 192.

11　Efraim Karsh and Inari Rautsi, *Saddam Hussein: A Political Biography*, p 214–16.

12　For a fine almost day-to-day chronology of the war, see the endpiece to James Piscatori, *Islamic Fundamentalism and the Gulf Crisis*, pp 209–44. See also Richard Schofield, *Kuwait and Iraq: Historical Claims and Territorial Disputes* (London: Royal Institute of International Affairs, 1991); and Walid Khalidi, *The Gulf Crisis: Origins and Consequences* (Washington, DC: Institute for Palestine Studies, 1990).

13　For a good discussion of the Christian basis and implications of just war, and an elucidation of the Augustinian principles, both as applied to conduct leading to war and conduct within war, see the US Bishops' 'Pastoral Letter on War and Peace 1983', reproduced as Chapter 5 of Jean Bethke Elshtain (ed), *Just War Theory* (Oxford: Blackwell, 1992).

14　A popular but good history of *jihad* and the historical meanings of holy war may be found in Karen Armstrong, *Holy War: The Crusades and Their Impact on Today's World* (London: Macmillan, 1988).

15　A.J. Coates, *The Ethics of War* (Manchester: Manchester University Press, 1997), p 206.

16　Richard Norman, *Ethics, Killing and War* (Cambridge: Cambridge University Press, 1995), p 240.

17　Michael Walzer, *Just and Unjust Wars* (New York: Basic Books, 1977).

18　*Ibid.*, p xxi.

19　Paul Ramsey, 'The Just War According to St. Augustine', in Jean Bethke Elshtain (ed), *Just War Theory*, p 16.

20　Dominique de Villepin, *Eloge des Voleurs de Feu* ('In Praise of the Stealers of Fire') (Paris: Gallimard, 2003).

21　Cited in Piers Morgan's Gulf War diary, excerpted in GQ, July 2003, p 131.

22　Evidence to the Hutton Inquiry, reported in the *Guardian*, 19 August 2003.

23 For a portrait of one such, Ahmad Chalabi, with no demonstrable Iraqi support, constituency or even public recognition, see David Rose, 'An Inconvenient Iraqi', *Vanity Fair*, January 2003. The war of favourites, i.e. which Iraqi candidate for a post-war position in government was favoured by which rival US agency, led to a rash of profiles and articles, not so much targeted at the general US public, but seemingly carefully placed to attract the allegiance and support of the intellectual and cultural communities.

24 For a short essay on this, see Stephen Chan, 'British and Commonwealth Actors in the 1980s', in Stephen Chan and Vivienne Jabri (eds), *Mediation in Southern Africa* (London: Macmillan, 1993).

Chapter 4. Other Lands and the Superhawks

1 See David Hirst's report in the *Guardian*, 21 August 2003.

2 Originally published in *Le Monde*. I am citing the English translation of Karim Pakradouni, 'Hafez al Assad - the Arab Bismarck', *Guardian Weekly*, 11 December 1983.

3 I have written earlier on this. See Stephen Chan, *Issues in International Relations: A View from Africa* (London: Macmillan, 1987), pp 146-7, 181-3.

4 There is a succinct summary of this in Paul B. Rich, 'The Construction of Ideologies in the Twentieth Century', in Chan and Wiener (eds), *Twentieth-Century International History*, pp 13-21. See especially p 19.

5 Efraim Karsh. 'From Ideological Zeal to Geopolitical Realism: The Islamic Republic and the Gulf', in Karsh (ed), *The Iran-Iraq War: Impact and Implications*, p 28.

6 Philip G. Philip, 'The Islamic Revolution in Iran: Its Impact on Foreign Policy', in Chan and Williams (eds), *Renegade States*, p 132.

7 Cited in Martin Kramer (ed), *Sh'ism, Resistance and Revolution* (Boulder: Westview, 1987), p 52.

8 Mahmoud Sariolghalam, 'Islamic Revolution of Iran: Sources of Change and Challenges for Adaptation', paper presented to the BISA Conference at the University of Kent, December 1989.

9 Asghar Schirazi, *The Constitution of Iran*, pp 173, and 202, notes 1 and 2.

10 Fred Halliday, *Islam and the Myth of Confrontation*, pp 46-7.

11 Ferdowsi, *Shahnameh: The Epic of the Kings* (Tehran: Yassavoli, 2001).

12 It is almost impossible to recount these contemporary legends without bursting into caricature. I first became aware of them in 1973, when I was president of the New Zealand university students. Without solicitation, dozens of North Korean books began arriving

at my office: endless volumes of speeches by the North Korean leader, Comrade Kim Il Sung, and mountainous coffee-table books of socialist-realist paintings depicting the heroic exploits of Kim against both Japanese and American aggressors alike. The style of painting was socialist-realist; the depiction of magical heroism, of God-like existentialism – i.e. not within absurdity but able to manipulate absurdity – was clearly antique, even if perversely so. I could not stop the flow of books and they followed me around the world, by now arriving in several languages. I finally shook them off by disappearing to Africa – to find a Lusaka drinking companion in the North Korean ambassador there, enjoying his cocktail recipe for immortality, derived he said from that of the ancient kings, and which consisted in random blends of ginseng and whiskey.

[13] For good histories, see Hazel Smith, 'The Democratic People's Republic of North Korea and Its Foreign Policy in the 1990s', in Chan and Williams (eds), *Renegade States*; Jon Halliday and Bruce Cumings, *Korea: The Unknown War* (New York: Pantheon, 1988).

[14] James E. Dougherty and Robert L. Pfaltzgraff Jr, *Contending Theories of International Relations* (New York: Harper & Row, 1981), p 369.

[15] Karl W. Deutsch, *The Analysis of International Relations* (Englewood Cliffs, NJ: Prentice-Hall, 1978), p 134.

[16] David Armstrong, *The Rise of the International Organisation* (London: Macmillan, 1982), p 60.

[17] Dougherty and Pfaltzgraff Jr, *Contending Theories of International Relations*, pp 369–70.

[18] Deutsche, *The Analysis of International Relations*, pp 86–8.

[19] Michael Walzer, *Just and Unjust Wars*, pp 117–24.

[20] One of the picturesque (but possibly untrue, certainly exaggerated) stories told to me by North Korean exiles was of an early *juche* exercise in which the 'Great Leader' had instructed a factory to produce trucks. No one had produced a truck before. A truck in working order was duly found, and the appointed truck-builders methodically dismantled it, studied all the parts and their connecting principles, then had duplicate parts built for the first prototype of a North Korean truck. The new truck was duly assembled in the right order – so it seemed – and the ignition switched on for its first ceremonial test run. Everything worked perfectly, except that the gear system had been misunderstood and the first *juche* truck could only move backwards. I was told various versions of this story over the years – always to hysterical laughter on the part of the narrators.

[21] Halliday and Cumings, *Korea: The Unknown War*, p 216.

[22] Ferdowsi, *Shahnameh*, Chapter XXXIV, p 181.

Chapter 5. The Veil of Good

[1] Ahmed Rashid uses the competition to establish an oil pipeline through Afghanistan, carrying oil south from the Transcaucasian fields, as the introductory and persistent backdrop to his superb work, *Taliban*.

[2] Most notably Fred Halliday, *The Making of the Second Cold War*.

[3] Robert Kagan, *Power and Paradise: America and Europe in the New World Order* (London: Atlantic, 2003).

[4] For some succinct accounts of this, see Chris Brown, *International Relations Theory: New Normative Approaches* (Hertfordshire: Harvester Wheatsheaf, 1992); and Janna Thompson, *Justice and World Order: A Philosophical Inquiry* (London: Routledge, 1992). Both authors seek to relate Kantian and other Enlightenment thought to contemporary international relations.

[5] Robert O. Keohane and Joseph S. Nye, *Power and Interdependence: World Politics in Transition* (Boston: Little Brown, 1977).

[6] Not that Susan Strange was by any means particularly sympathetic or supportive of US hegemony, or of early regime theory in which the US was not identified as a hegemon. See Tooze and May (eds), *Authority and Markets*, e.g. Chapters 9 and 15.

[7] Kagan, *Power and Paradise*, p 61. Here Kagan is citing EU Commissioner Chris Patten.

[8] This is Robert Cooper's *Observer* article, 7 April 2002, cited in Kagan, *Power and Paradise*, p 74.

[9] Kagan, *Power and Paradise*, p 81.

[10] *Ibid.*, p 97.

[11] There is a huge literature on the question of aid and the vexed methodologies of aid, but see Jean Dreze and Amartya Sen, *Hunger and Public Action* (Oxford: Clarendon, 1990). I tried to make my own early notes on the debate in the first half of Stephen Chan, *Social Development in Africa Today: Some Radical Proposals* (Lewiston, NJ: Edwin Mellen, 1991).

[12] For a comment on this in the early stages of the War on Terror, see Richard Johnson, 'Defending Ways of Life: The Anti-Terrorist Rhetorics of Bush and Blair', *Theory, Culture & Society*, Autumn 2002.

[13] Susan Sontag, *Regarding the Pain of Others* (London: Hamish Hamilton, 2003).

[14] I should point out an interesting application of agreed doctrine in conventional war. In the war over Bangladesh, Indian and Pakistani generals, both trained at Sandhurst, followed exactly the same field

manuals and procedures. Theoretically each knew or should have known what the other was going to do. This was true, but the Indians won because they simply did it faster.

[15] Hans Kung and Helmut Schmidt (eds), *A Global Ethic and Global Responsibilities: Two Declarations* (London: SCM Press, 1998). See also Stephen Chan, 'Rorty as Shadow Warrior: Hans Kung and a Global Ethic', *Review of International Studies*, Vol. 25, No. 3 (1999).

[16] I have tried to make some modest effort here: Stephen Chan, Peter Mandaville and Roland Bleiker, *The Zen of International Relations: IR Theory from East to West* (London: Palgrave Macmillan, 2001); Stephen Chan, *Towards a Multicultural Roshamon Paradigm in International Relations* (Tampere: Tampere Peace Research Institute, 1996).

Chapter 6. In Praise of Cheese-Eating Surrender Monkeys

[1] Illustrating the extent of international interest in 9/11 and the world events it precipitated, I am here using Michael Duffy's 'Could September 11 Happen Again?', a widely enough syndicated feature, but the extensive article I am citing covers three pages of Zambia's *Post* newspaper, 28 July 2003.

[2] Robert Jungk, *Brighter than 1000 Suns* (Harmondsworth: Penguin, 1960).

[3] André Malraux, *Anti-Memoirs* (New York: Henry Holt, 1967), p 181.

[4] *Ibid.*, p 222.

BIBLIOGRAPHY

Afrasiabi, Kaveh L., 'The Contest of Civilizations and Interreligious Dialogue', *The Iranian Journal of International Affairs*, XI:3 (1999)

—, 'On the "Clash of Civilizations"', *Telos*, 115 (2000)

Ahmed, Akbar S., *Postmodernism and Islam: Predicament and Promise* (London: Routledge, 1992)

Anwar, Raja, *The Tragedy of Afghanistan: A First-Hand Account* (London: Verso, 1988)

Armstrong, David, *The Rise of the International Organisation* (London: Macmillan, 1982)

Armstrong, Karen, *Holy War: The Crusades and Their Impact on Today's World* (London: Macmillan, 1988)

Attar, Faridu'd-Din, *The Speech of the Birds* (Cambridge: Islamic Texts Society, 1998)

Bacon, Paul, 'The End of History and the First Man of the Twenty-First Century', in Stephen Chan and Jarrod Wiener (eds), *Twentieth-Century International History* (London: I.B. Tauris, 1999)

Bailey, Sydney D., *Four Arab–Israeli Wars and the Peace Process* (London: Macmillan, 1990)

Blomstrom, Magnus and Bjorn Hettne, *Development Theory in Transition: The Dependency Debate and Beyond – Third World Responses* (London: Zed, 1984)

Brodie, Bernard, *War and Politics* (New York: Macmillan, 1973)

Brown, Chris, *International Relations Theory: New Normative Approaches* (Hertfordshire: Harvester Wheatsheaf, 1992)

— (ed), *Political Restructuring in Europe: Ethical Perspectives* (London: Routledge, 1994)

Buck, Joan Juliet, 'France's Prophet Provocateur', *Vanity Fair*, January 2003

Campbell, David, *National Deconstruction: Violence, Identity and Justice in Bosnia* (Minneapolis: University of Minnesota Press, 1998)

Chan, Stephen, *Issues in International Relations: A View from Africa* (London: Macmillan, 1987)

——, *Exporting Apartheid: Foreign Policies in Southern Africa 1978–1988* (London: Macmillan, 1990)

——, *Social Development in Africa Today: Some Radical Proposals* (Lewiston, NJ: Edwin Mellen, 1991)

—— and Vivienne Jabri (eds), *Mediation in Southern Africa* (London: Macmillan, 1993)

—— and Andrew J. Williams (eds), *Renegade States: The Evolution of Revolutionary Foreign Policy* (Manchester: Manchester University Press, 1994)

——, *Towards a Multicultural Roshamon Paradigm in International Relations* (Tampere: Tampere Peace Research Institute, 1996)

——, 'Too Neat and Under-Thought a World Order: Huntington and Civilisations', *Millennium*, 26:1 (1997)

—— and Dominic Powell, 'Reform, Insurgency and Counter-Insurgency in Afghanistan', in Paul B. Rich and Richard Stubbs (eds), *The Counter-Insurgent State: Guerilla Warfare and State Building in the Twentieth Century* (London: Macmillan, 1997)

—— and Jarrod Wiener (eds), *Twentieth-Century International History* (London: I.B. Tauris, 1999)

——, 'Rorty as Shadow Warrior: Hans Kung and a Global Ethic', *Review of International Studies*, Vol. 25, No. 3 (1999)

——, Peter Mandaville and Roland Bleiker, *The Zen of International Relations: IR Theory from East to West* (London: Palgrave Macmillan, 2001)

——, 'Reliving the Boxer Uprising; or, the Restricted Meaning of Civilisation', in Peter Mandaville and Andrew Williams (eds), *Meaning and International Relations* (London: Routledge, 2003)

Chubin, Shahram and Charles Tripp, *Iran and Iraq at War* (London: I.B. Tauris, 1988)

Coates, A.J., *The Ethics of War* (Manchester: Manchester University Press, 1997)

Cviic, Christopher, *Remaking the Balkans* (London: Royal Institute of International Affairs, 1991)

Dalby, Simon, *Creating the Second Cold War: The Discourse of Politics* (London: Pinter, 1990)

Dasgupta, Partha, *An Inquiry into Well-Being and Destitution* (Oxford: Oxford University Press, 1993)

Davis, John, *Libyan Politics: Tribe and Revolution* (London: I.B. Tauris, 1987)

Dawisha, Adeed (ed), *Islam in Foreign Policy* (Cambridge: Cambridge University Press, 1985)

Der Derian, James, *Antidiplomacy: Spies, Terror, Speed, and War* (Oxford: Blackwell, 1992)

Deutsch, Karl W., *The Analysis of International Relations* (Englewood Cliffs, NJ: Prentice-Hall, 1978)

Doran, Michael Scott, 'Gods and Monsters', *Guardian*, 8 December 2001

Dougherty, James E. and Robert L. Pfaltzgraff Jr, *Contending Theories of International Relations* (New York: Harper & Row, 1981)

Dreze, Jean and Amartya Sen, *Hunger and Public Action* (Oxford: Clarendon, 1990)

Elshtain, Jean Bethke (ed), *Just War Theory* (Oxford: Blackwell, 1992)

Farouk-Sluglett, Marion and Peter Sluglett, *Iraq since 1958: From Revolution to Dictatorship* (London: I.B. Tauris, 2001)

Ferdowsi, *Shahnameh: The Epic of the Kings* (Tehran: Yassavoli, 2001)

Finkielkraut, Alain, *The Crime of Being Born* (Zagreb: Ceres, 1997)

Foucault, Michel, *Politics, Philosophy, Culture: Interviews and Other Writings 1977–1984* (ed Lawrence D. Kritzman) (New York: Routledge, 1988)

Fukuyama, Francis, 'The End of History?', *The National Interest*, 16 (Summer 1989)

——, *The End of History and the Last Man* (London: Penguin, 1992)

Groom, A.J.R., *British Thinking about Nuclear Weapons* (London: Pinter, 1974)

Halliday, Fred, *The Making of the Second Cold War* (London: Verso, 1983)

——, *Cold War, Third World: An Essay on Soviet–American Relations* (London: Hutchinson Radius, 1989)

——, *Islam and the Myth of Confrontation: Religion and Politics in the Middle East* (London: I.B. Tauris, 1996)

Halliday, Jon and Bruce Cumings, *Korea: The Unknown War* (New York: Pantheon, 1988)

Hibbert, Sir Reginald, *The Kosovo Question: Origins, Present Complications and Prospects* (London: David Davies Memorial Institute Occasional Paper 11, May 1999)

Hiro, Dilip, *The Longest War: The Iran–Iraq Military Conflict* (London: Grafton, 1989)

Hobson, John M., *The Wealth of States: A Comparative Sociology of International Economic and Political Change* (Cambridge: Cambridge University Press, 1997)

Hoffman, Mark (ed), *UK Arms Control in the 1990s* (Manchester: Manchester University Press, 1990)

Hollis, Martin and Steve Smith, *Explaining and Understanding in International Relations* (Oxford: Clarendon, 1991)

Hourani, Albert, Philip S. Khoury and Mary C. Wilson (eds), *The Modern Middle East: A Reader* (Berkeley: University of California Press, 1993)

Hroub, Khaled, *Hamas: Political Thought and Practice* (Washington, DC: Institute for Palestine Studies, 2000)

Huntington, Samuel P., 'The Clash of Civilizations?', *Foreign Affairs*, 72 (Summer 1993)

——, *The Clash of Civilizations and the Remaking of World Order* (New York: Simon & Schuster, 1996)

——, 'The Clash of Civilizations – A Response', *Millennium*, 26:1 (1997)

Johnson, Richard, 'Defending Ways of Life: The Anti-Terrorist Rhetorics of Bush and Blair', *Theory, Culture & Society*, Autumn 2002

Jungk, Robert, *Brighter than 1000 Suns* (Harmondsworth: Penguin, 1960)

Kagan, Robert, *Power and Paradise: America and Europe in the New World Order* (London: Atlantic, 2003)

Kahn, Herman, *On Thermonuclear War* (Princeton: Princeton University Press, 1961)

——, *Thinking about the Unthinkable* (London: Weidenfeld & Nicolson, 1962)

——, *On Escalation: Metaphors and Scenarios* (London: Pall Mall, 1965)

Karsh, Efraim (ed), *The Iran–Iraq War: Impact and Implications* (London: Macmillan, 1989)

—— and Inari Rautsi, *Saddam Hussein: A Political Biography* (New York: Free Press, 1991)

Kaufmann, William W., *Military Policy and National Security* (Princeton: Princeton University Press, 1972)

Keddie, Nikki R., 'Iranian Revolutions in Comparative Perspective', in Albert Hourani, Philip S. Khoury and Mary C. Wilson (eds), *The Modern Middle East: A Reader* (Berkeley: University of California Press, 1993)

Kennedy, Paul, *The Rise and Fall of the Great Powers* (London: Unwin Hyman, 1988)

Kennedy, Robert F., *13 Days* (London: Macmillan, 1969)

Keohane, Robert O. and Joseph S. Nye, *Power and Interdependence: World Politics in Transition* (Boston: Little Brown, 1977)

Khalidi, Tarif (ed), *The Muslim Jesus: Sayings and Stories in Islamic Literature* (Cambridge, MA: Harvard University Press, 2001)

Khalidi, Walid, *The Gulf Crisis: Origins and Consequences* (Washington, DC: Institute for Palestine Studies, 1990)

Khusraw, Nasir (ed & trans Faquir M. Hunzai), *Knowledge and Liberation: A Treatise on Philosophical Theology* (London: I.B. Tauris, 1999)

Kissinger, Henry, *A World Restored: Metternich, Castlereagh and the Problems of Peace 1812–22* (London: Weidenfeld & Nicolson, 1957)

Knorr, Klaus and James N. Rosenau (eds), *Contending Approaches to International Politics* (Princeton: Princeton University Press, 1969)

Kramer, Martin (ed), *Sh'ism, Resistance and Revolution* (Boulder: Westview, 1987)

Kung, Hans and Helmut Schmidt (eds), *A Global Ethic and Global Responsibilities: Two Declarations* (London: SCM Press, 1998)

Kuo-kang Shao, *Zhou Enlai and the Foundations of Chinese Foreign Policy* (London: Macmillan, 1996)

Lawrence, T.E., *Seven Pillars of Wisdom* (London: Penguin, 1962)

Levi, Primo, *If Not Now, When?* (London: Abacus, 1987)

Ling, L.H.M., *Conquest Desire: Postcolonial Learning between Asia and the West* (New York: St Martin's Press, 2001)

Madelung, Wilfred and Toby Mayer (trans & eds), *Struggling with the Philosopher: Muhammad b. 'Abd al-Karim al-Shahrastani's Kitab al-Musara'a* (London: I.B. Tauris, 2001)

Malraux, André, *Anti-Memoirs* (New York: Henry Holt, 1967)

Martin, Laurence, *The Two-Edged Sword* (London: Weidenfeld & Nicolson, 1982)

Mohammadi, Ali and Muhammad Ahsan, *Globalisation or Recolonisation? The Muslim World in the 21st Century* (London: Ta-Ha, 2002)

Nicholson, Michael, *Rationality and the Analysis of International Conflict* (Cambridge: Cambridge University Press, 1992)

Norman, Richard, *Ethics, Killing and War* (Cambridge: Cambridge University Press, 1995)

O'Neill, Robert and David N. Schwartz (eds), *Hedley Bull on Arms Control* (London: Macmillan, 1987)

Pagels, Elaine, *The Gnostic Gospels* (New York: Random House, 1979)

——, *The Origin of Satan* (London: Allen Lane, 1996)

Pakradouni, Karim, 'Hafez al Assad - the Arab Bismarck', *Guardian Weekly*, 11 December 1983

Peters, Joan, *From Time Immemorial: The Origins of the Arab–Jewish Conflict over Palestine* (London: Michael Joseph, 1984)

Philip, Philip G., 'The Islamic Revolution in Iran: Its Impact on Foreign Policy', in Stephen Chan and Andrew J. Williams (eds), *Renegade States: The Evolution of Revolutionary Foreign Policy* (Manchester: Manchester University Press, 1994)

Piscatori, James (ed), *Islamic Fundamentalisms and the Gulf Crisis* (Chicago: American Academy of Arts and Sciences, 1991)

Prebisch, Raul, *The Economic Development of Latin America and its Principal Problems* (New York: UN, 1950)

Rahnema, Ali, *An Islamic Utopian: A Political Biography of Ali Shari'ati* (London: I.B. Tauris, 2000)

Ramet, Sabrina P., *Nationalism and Federalism in Yugoslavia 1962–1991* (Bloomington: Indiana University Press, 1992)

Rapoport, Anatol, 'Introduction' to Karl Von Clausewitz, *On War* (London: Pelican, 1968)

Rashid, Ahmed, *Taliban: Islam, Oil and the New Great Game in Central Asia* (London: I.B. Tauris, 2001)

Rich, Paul B., 'The Construction of Ideologies in the Twentieth Century', in Stephen Chan and Jarrod Wiener (eds), *Twentieth-Century International History* (London: I.B. Tauris, 1999)

Rose, David, 'An Inconvenient Iraqi', *Vanity Fair*, January 2003

Said, Edward W., *Covering Islam* (London: Routledge and Kegan Paul, 1981)

—, *Reflections on Exile* (London: Granta, 2000)

—, 'A Window on the World', *The Guardian* (Review), 2 August 2003

—, *Orientalism* (London: Penguin, 2003)

Sariolghalam, Mahmoud, 'Islamic Revolution of Iran: Sources of Change and Challenges for Adaptation', paper presented to the BISA Conference at the University of Kent, December 1989

—, 'The Determinants of Iraqi Foreign Policy Behaviour in the 1980s', in Stephen Chan and Andrew J. Williams (eds), *Renegade States: The Evolution of Revolutionary Foreign Policy* (Manchester: Manchester University Press, 1994)

Schirazi, Asghar, *The Constitution of Iran: Politics and the State in the Islamic Republic* (London: I.B. Tauris, 1998)

Schofield, Richard, *Kuwait and Iraq: Historical Claims and Territorial Disputes* (London: Royal Institute of International Affairs, 1991)

Smith, Hazel, 'The Democratic People's Republic of North Korea and Its Foreign Policy in the 1990s', in Stephen Chan and Andrew J. Williams (eds), *Renegade States: The Evolution of Revolutionary Foreign Policy* (Manchester: Manchester University Press, 1994)

Sontag, Susan, *Regarding the Pain of Others* (London: Hamish Hamilton, 2003)

Sowell, Thomas, *Race and Culture: A World View* (New York: Basic Books, 1994)

Spence, Jonathan D., *The Chan's Great Continent: China in Western Minds* (New York: W.W. Norton, 1998)

Sreberny-Mohammadi, Annabelle and Ali Mohammadi, *Small Media, Big Revolution: Communication, Culture, and the Iranian Revolution* (Minneapolis: University of Minnesota Press, 1994)

Stone, Brian (trans), *Sir Gawain and the Green Knight* (London: Penguin, 1959)

Thompson, E.P., Mary Kaldor, et al, *Mad Dogs: The US Raids on Libya* (London: Pluto, 1986)

Thompson, Janna, *Justice and World Order: A Philosophical Inquiry* (London: Routledge, 1992)

Tooze, Roger and Christopher May, *Authority and Markets: Susan Strange's Writings on International Political Economy* (London: Palgrave Macmillan, 2002)

Tripp, Charles A., *A Political History of Iraq* (Cambridge: Cambridge University Press, 2000)

Usuki, E., 'An End to the "End of History" Debates', *International Relations* (Japanese-language journal), 99 (1992)

Villepin, Dominique de, *Eloge des Voleurs de Feu* ('In Praise of the Stealers of Fire') (Paris: Gallimard, 2003)

Walzer, Michael, *Just and Unjust Wars* (New York: Basic Books, 1977)

White, Ralph K., *Nobody Wanted War* (New York: Doubleday, 1968)

Yee, Herbert S., 'The Three-World Theory and Post-Mao China's Global Strategy', *International Affairs*, 59:2 (1983)

INDEX